GREEN HEADS & BLACK BASS

60 Years of Hunting & Fishing in South Louisiana

by

J.A. "Bud" Oliver

Sorrel Publishing Company
1878 Chevelle Drive
Baton Rouge, LA 70806
(225) 925-8993

First Edition 1999

All Rights Reserved, including the right of reproduction in whole or in part in any form.

Copyright © 1999 J.A. "Bud" Oliver

Manufactured in the United States of America

ISBN: 0-9671048-0-7

DEDICATION

I want to dedicate this book to my wife of 54 years, Shirley, and to my five children, Richard, David, Carolyn, Nancy, and Patricia, to my parents, Rock and Annie Oliver, to my "in laws", George and Evelyn Guilbeau, to my granddaughters, Amy & Ashley Thompson, to my sons-in-law, "Chet" Thompson and Robert Hall, my grandchild "on the way", and last, but certainly not least, to all of my dear friends with whom I have hunted and fished and that participated in the events recounted in this book.

CONTENTS

Preface vii

Chapter 1: HUNTING
    A Lucky Mallard Hunt 2
    A Hunt at Jim's "Couzan's" Camp 5
    Hunting with a Former Lt. Governor of LA 7
    Back Yard Mallards..10
    "Jelly Bean" Hunt 12
    A Real Good Outing 16
    Another Hunt at the Mouth of the Mississippi River   20
    High Water Duck Hunting 22
    Wading - Another Means of Taking Ducks 24
    Sounds from a Duck Blind 29
    A Rice Field Duck Hunt 30
    First Quail Hunting Trip 32
    "Jelly Bean" Hunt #2..33
    "Rusty" 35
    "Dan" 38
    Obeying Hunting Rules & Regulations 39

Chapter II: FISHING
    Fishing Holes Around 44
    My First Fishing Trip 47
    Old Fishing Equipment and Lures 52
    Fishing Trips - No Motor 58
    Fishing Trip to Buzzard Bayou 61
    Other Ways to Catch Bass 64
    Night Fishing for Bass 69
    Hooked Fisherman (About Lake Sutton) 72
    Catching White Bass 75

Chapter III: OUTDOOR ARTICLES
    The Atchafalaya Basin 78

"The Old Swamper" 80
Swamp Neighbors 88
Texas Green Horns to the Swamp 95
Another Hunt at Point Au Fer 100
A Sad Experience 104
Duck Hunting Fever 105
15 Banded Ducks 106
Young & Foolish 111
Sights and Sounds of the Swamps 113
A Near Disaster on the Mississippi River 115
Rescue on the Red River 118
Another Outdoor Water Sport 120

Chapter IV: SAFETY
Gun Safety 124
Boating Safety 126
Alcohol 127
Hazardous Fishing and Hunting Places 128

Chapter V: ODD HAPPENINGS
Odd Catches 133
Spike's Bay 136
The Big One that Got Away 138
Could Have Been Worse 140
An Odd Retrieve 141

Chapter VI: HUMOROUS HAPPENINGS
Nothing Else to Hold On To 143
Inflating a Mae West Life Preserver to See If It Works 144
Using Spray Paint as Mosquito Dope 145
Be Sure to Bring the Pork Rind 146
Upside Down Long Johns 148
I'm Glad You Didn't Kill That Deer 149
"Louis's Duck Hunt - A Broken Gun" 151
Mr. Mack's Quail Hunt 153

Canadian "Goose" Fever ………………………………...156
Uncle Alcide's "Talk" With His Dog…………………...157
Alarm Clock "Snafu" ……………………………………160

Chapter VII: CAMPING
My Camping Box ………………………………162
Camp and "Lean To" Building ……………………….164
Camp Chores ……………………………………...…...167
Worst Camping Setup………………………..…………172
Worst Camping Trip ……………………………………174
The Three "Unwise" Men ……………………………...177

Chapter VIII:- INSTRUCTIONAL
Ducks & Duck Calling ………………………………180
Wing Shooting ……………………………………...181
Shotguns and Shells …………………………………183
Training A Retriever ………………………………...184
Getting There the Hard Way ……………………….187
Building Different Types of Duck Blinds …………..190
Blind Placement ……………………………………..198
Push Poles ……………………………………………199
Swamp Mud Shoes …………………………………..200
Getting Out of a Mud Hole …………………………202
Boat Building ………………………………………..203
Launching a Boat at a Difficult Landing …………..206

Chapter IX: INSPIRATIONAL
Solitude ………………………………………………208
Devotion ……………………………………………..210
Last Day of a Season ………………………………..211
Last Hunt of a Season ……………………………….212
"Days Gone By ………………………………………213
Reflections …………………………………………...214

Chapter X: CAMP COOKING
- Camp Stew 217
- Corn Soup 218
- Fried Fish & Fried Potatoes 219
- Peas & Eggs 219
- Smothered Potatoes & Sausage 220
- Venison Tenderloin 220
- Venison Back Strap 221
- Crawfish or Shrimp Stew 221
- Pressure Pot Duck 222
- Baking Biscuits with No Oven 223
- Ham Steak & Red Eye Gravy 223
- Rice 224
- Roux 224
- Camp Chili 224

EPILOGUE...226

> The stories and information contained herein are the views of the author. Use discretion when attempting to duplicate any instructions contained in this book.

PREFACE

I was born March 26, 1923, in Baton Rouge, LA. My father was Rock Oliver, a barber by trade, and my mother was Annie C. Oliver, a homemaker and business woman.

I am a true Baton Rouge "native", residing here all of my life, with the exception of 3 years I spent in the Army - 2 years "overseas" in the South Pacific and the occupation of Japan.

I attended school in Baton Rouge and graduated from Baton Rouge High School, where I played football for 2 years.
I completed a 400 hour course in Mechanics at LSU, as well as a Mechanical Drawing course at a local vo-tech school.

In 1944, I married Shirley Rose Guilbeau Oliver and we raised five children, Richard, David, Carolyn, Nancy and Patricia. They all reside locally.

My father-in-law was George G. Guilbeau, a farmer and cattleman, and my mother-in-law was Evelyn G. Guilbeau, a homemaker and school teacher.

Our oldest daughter is married to "Chet" Thompson, and they have 2 daughters, Amy and Ashley.

Patricia, our youngest daughter, is married to Robert H. Hall, and they are expecting their first child in March.

After completing my Army service, I worked for 17 years at Ethyl Corporation, then was employed by H.E. Wiese and Jacobs Engineering for a total of 17 years. I retired in 1981 from the position of Director of Construction Services, at the early age of 58.

At an early age, I was introduced to the out of doors by my father, and I have hunted and fished ever since. As a boy, I always had a BB gun, a Daisy, and when I was a teenager I graduated to a 22, it was a Remington pump. After watching a demonstration of a Remington trick shot artist, I also tried some of his tricks and got to be pretty proficient, proficient enough to hit a penny that I'd tossed in the air with a 22. And believe it or not I can still do it today, but it takes more shots. I hope this book will help someone be a better duck hunter or a better bass fisherman and make everyone aware of the great strides that have been made in improving our sporting goods and outdoor equipment. And last but not least, I need to add that a friend of mine once said, "There are good duck hunters and there are bad duck hunters, but there are no expert duck hunters...", and that also goes for fishermen. When you think that you have mastered the art, you'll go out and get skunked. So, don't ever give up, just keep trying and you'll eventually succeed.

I decided to write this book in hopes that it will give a novice some help in things they may encounter in the field or on the water. I also hope this collection of stories will bring back memories to some of the older hunters and fishermen, and maybe, bring a smile to their faces when they recall similar instances.

I believe you will find this book useful, informative, entertaining and humorous, as well as a few sad moments - it is, however, all factual.

-The Author
J.A. "Bud" Oliver
(1/1/99)

The author's den.

The author's first hunting & fishing license and duck stamp, $1.00 each!

HUNTING

A LUCKY MALLARD HUNT

I was on vacation from a local refinery that I worked for in the late 50's, duck season was open and we had been making a long trip to Grand Lake, but weren't having much luck. My hunting partner, Bill Lyon, called and said, "Bud, I hear there are some ducks in the old swamp out from Charlie Henson's Landing. You want to give it a try?". I said, "Sure, Bill, let's go scouting this afternoon."

Well, sure enough, we left Baton Rouge around midday, drove to Bayou Sorrel, and launched at Henson's Landing. Charlie Henson's landing was the only landing at Bayou Sorrel. The launching fee was $0.75, but if you gave Charlie a dollar, he would always say without hesitation, "You don't want your change do you?". We would have a good laugh and tell him, "No, that's your tip!". Bill had a 14' bateau with an 18 hp Evinrude on it. We talked to Charlie and he said that some of the fisherman had been seeing ducks off of the "9 mile canal".

Well, we shoved off and proceeded down the "9 mile canal". It was named this because it was 9 miles to the Atchafalaya River from the levee.

We had only brought our guns as this was an exploring trip. We were easing along at about 10 mph and were about ½ of the way down the "9 mile canal" when I saw a flight of ducks cross the canal up ahead, but flying very high.

I told Bill to cut the motor so we could see where they were going. He cut the motor and, lo and behold, just next to our boat about 100 mallards burst through the trees and, boy, did we get excited. We tried to get the bateau into the woods, but it was too thick. We tried to hunt from the edge, but we were not hidden and therefore, did not get a shot. Bill said, "Let's come back in the morning with our pirogue and some decoys." We marked the spot, and the next morning we were there well before daylight with a pirogue, a sack of decoys and a machete.

We paddled in about 200 yards, leaving the bateau on the canal. We found a downed willow that was still growing and pulled our pirogue in amongst the branches, using the machete to clear the obstruction away.

As daylight approached, those mallards started pouring in, and it didn't take long to limit out. We stashed the pirogue and came out. I told Bill that I wanted to come back in the morning, but he said that he had promised some fellows to go to North Louisiana on a rabbit hunt, however, he would leave his bateau and motor at Charlie's and I could find someone else to come back with me.

Well, that's exactly what I did. I called a friend and the next morning we came back and did real good. If we hadn't limited out by 9:00 a.m., we would have paddled the swamp, taking turns shooting and getting our limit by jump shooting.

We also started bringing a couple of casting rods and several spinner baits, and when we would limit out early, we would stash the pirogue and put up the guns and try to catch a few bass in some of the holes we knew of in the swamp - Queen Lake, Berry Lake, Spikes Bay and others.

Several times, we came out to the landing with a limit of mallards and a limit of black bass - what a wonderful outing.

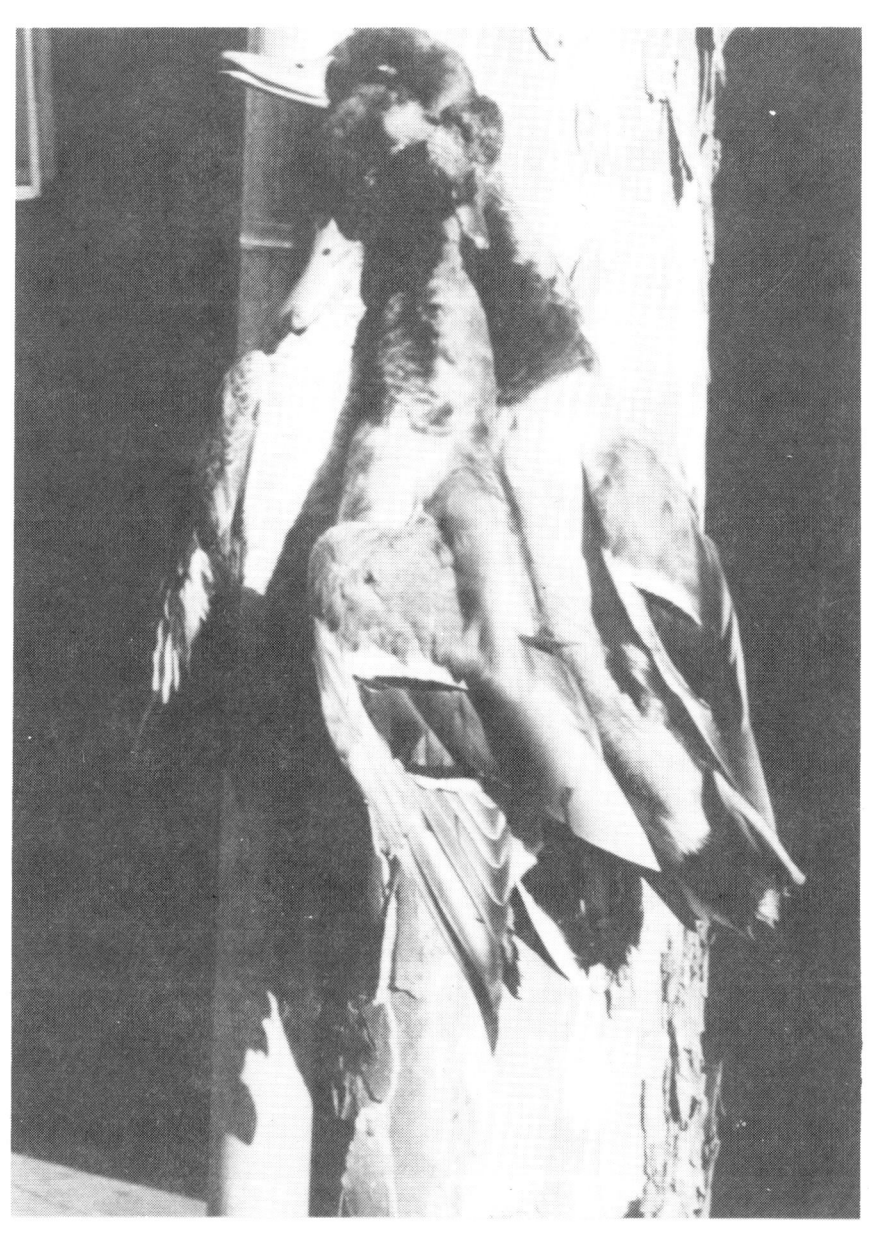

Swamp mallards - a good hunt!

A HUNT AT JIM'S "COUZAN'S" CAMP

On one of the large construction projects I worked, I became familiar with a sub-contractor who, like me, was a duck hunter.

He kept telling me about a cousin who had a floating camp and a lease in the marsh. We talked about making a hunt, but never did get around to make it for a couple of years, but finally, we made plans. This was about 1970, and we got ready to go. Jim had an aluminum boat, about 16' long and a 35 HP Evinrude.

We left Baton Rouge early one morning, as we had a long way to go, an of course, my dog, "Rusty" was with us.

We stopped in Houma, LA, for provisions and gas as it was a pretty long boat ride and we were going to spend the night. We launched the boat at Theriot, LA, and proceeded down that canal to Lake Decade, quite a large body of water, but we would skirt the northern tip of the lake for a coupe of miles and go into a canal where his "couzan" had a camp. He always called his cousin, "Couzan", the French word for "cousin".

We got to the floating camp and it was tied up very near a weir. We off loaded our gear and as it was still early afternoon, I wanted to make a hunt. Jim didn't feel up to it, but he told me I could go.

We climbed a ladder to the top of the house boat and Jim pointed the blind out to me. By the way, "Couzan" was to come later.

I got one of the pirogues and with "Rusty", my retriever, pulled over the weir and proceeded to paddled about ¾ of a mile to the blind. The ducks started flying and I made a good afternoon hunt. Neither Jim or "Couzan" came out to the blind, but stayed instead at the camp, having a few cocktails. We had supper, but I ended up doing the cooking, and then, we went to bed.

The little camp was quite comfortable and I slept as good as expected, as I don't sleep too good in strange surroundings.

I woke up early and lay awake waiting for the owner or Jim to get up. Pretty soon, I could see the sky being to get bright and I called out to Jim and asked him if he was going to hunt. He said that we had plenty of time. I asked if he minded if I got up, made the coffee and started to get ready. He said that would be fine.

I made coffee and then told him that we better get going, however, I got the same response, "we have plenty of time". I said, "Do you mind if I go on ahead?" He simply responded, "Go ahead".

I hurriedly got dressed and took off. Having to paddle that ¾ mile and while I was paddling, ducks were all over the sky. I got to the blind and in a short time, I had 10 gadwal drakes which was the limit. As I was paddling out, I saw Jim and "Couzan" coming. They were in the mud boat. They turned around and towed me back and didn't hunt at all.

I gave them the six ducks I killed that afternoon and my 10 duck limit of that morning, and they were satisfied.

When we got to the weir, the tide was flowing out and a man and his wife were catching red fish. They were using shad rigs with a small piece of shrimp on the hook. The fish were biting so good, they had to take one of the lures off of the shad rig as those big red fish were too much to handle catching 2 at a time. The fisherman had a tub full of fish.

They gave us a few shrimp and we used a couple of rods at the camp and we also joined in the fun of catching the red fish.

By noon, we had loaded up and were ready to come home. I believe that "Couzan" was loaded up also.! I don't believe I have to tell you, but that was the first and last hunt that I made down there!

HUNTING WITH A FORMER LIEUTENANT GOVERNOR OF THE STATE OF LOUISIANA

I had occasion one day to share a duck blind with former Lieutenant Governor C.C. "Taddy" Aycock. This was in 1974, I believe.

I was a guest of my neighbor and hunting companion, "Cub" Roberts at Mr. McGee's houseboat at Point Au Fer, Louisiana, in St. Mary Parish (south of Morgan City, LA) This is near the Atchafalaya Bay and the Gulf of Mexico.

"Taddy" was also a frequent guest, however, I had never hunted with him. "Taddy" would entertain us after supper with tales of Louisiana politics, especially when we were having our "social hour" before bed time.

He would tell some hilarious tales of different politicians and some of the happenings when he was in office. Also, stories of preceding administrations and of administrations that followed his retirement. He was quite amusing.

He told of one governor who had made a campaign promise to a school board. Well, he did not keep the promise after he was elected to office, so a committee was formed to confront him about this. By the way, this story was confirmed by one of the committee members that I had occasion to meet at a later date while I served as a member of a jury.

The "committee members", I believe, consisted of 6 or 8 people, who had made an appointment to meet the Governor at the mansion. They all had their little notebooks and speeches ready to really chastise the governor. They were graciously received at the Governor's Mansion and were made to feel "welcome". Coffee was served, then the Governor appeared. He said, "Gentleman, I know why you are here and I want to tell you that I lied to you and if you will be patient I will try to fulfill my promise, but if you try to pressure me, you'll never get what you want as long as I'm in office."

That took the wind out of the committee's sails - they folded their notebooks and went home. We all had a good laugh at that story, especially the punch line, "...I lied to you...".

Well, getting back to the events of the hunt, "Taddy" told Mr. McGee that he would like to hunt the next morning with me. He wanted to see my retriever, "Rusty", work. "Cub" always called "Rusty" the man in the brown suit as he was a chocolate Labrador.

Mr. McGee said that it would be a fine arrangement, so the next morning, "Taddy" and I got in my boat for the short ride to a weir where we tied up and walked over the ridge to the pirogue. Once in the pirogue, we paddled a short distance and pulled the pirogue up on a little island where we had made a blind in the roseau cane. "Rusty" jumped enthusiastically out of the pirogue and took his morning constitutional and then, we were ready to hunt.

As luck would have it, the ducks were flying and decoying, and "Rusty" was being "worked" pretty good when "Taddy" shot a pintail drake that was a flying cripple that hit the water more than a 100 yards away and immediately keeled over dead. There was a pretty good wind blowing and the duck was blowing away from us.

"Taddy" said, "Bud, he will never get that duck...". As you know, a dog's eyes are just a few inches over the water when swimming and when there is wave action, it is hard for a dog to see a dead duck. He said, "You'll have to go get it with the pirogue...". I replied, quite confidently, " 'Taddy', that duck will soon be in this blind." I ordered "Rusty" to fetch and, as you know, the marsh is flat so when you stand up you can be seen for a quite a distance. I stood up and kept ordering "Rusty" "back", and he knew when I sent him out there was a duck out there.

The wind was still carrying the duck further and "Rusty" was still going "back", but was going too far to the right of the bird. So, "Taddy" asked, "What are you going to do now?" I replied matter of factly, "I'll show you." I let "Rusty" swim past the duck. When he was about 10 yards past the duck, I whistled to him and gave him a hand signal to turn left. In a couple of minutes, I saw him catch the scent of the duck. "Rusty" picked up the bird and started swimming back towards the blind with it in his mouth.

"Taddy" shook my hand and said, "Bud, that is about as pretty a job of retrieving as I've ever seen, and I've seen many retrievers work."

"Taddy" passed away a few years ago. He was a good sportsman.

"Rusty" making a long retrieve

BACK YARD MALLARDS

One Monday afternoon, when I reported for work at a local refinery, my co-worker and friend approached me and said, "Bud, how would you like to make a duck hunt right here in our back yard?" I said, "What in the world are you talking about?" He said, "This weekend, I saw a great many ducks not 10 miles from the city limits of Baton Rouge."

Well, that really got my interest as we had been making a long run up the Red River of about 75 miles by car plus a long boat ride.

He went on to explain he had taken a boat ride to Spanish Lake with a friend and saw a large concentration of mallards.

As we were on the 3-11 shift, we decided to go to Spanish Lake the following morning. My friend, Joe, had a small bateau with a 15 HP motor and I had about 2 dozen decoys. So, very early, he picked me up and we traveled south of Baton Rouge to a little stream called "Alligator Bayou" where there was a boat launch.

It was a short boat ride of about 3 miles to the lake and you could motor through a cut into the lake. We didn't have a blind, but the indigo weeds were about 8 feet tall and they were loaded with seeds. We put the decoys out and pulled our boat back under the indigo bushes and had a pretty good natural blind.

When daylight came, those mallards started to pour in. They really went for those indigo seeds. Those were the easiest ducks to decoy that I have ever seen. When we would knock down a couple and pole out to get them, those seeds would rain down in the boat. My friend, Joe, had a pump gun and several times, the seeds jammed the action.

We went several times that week and then, it was the end of the first split of the duck season. During the 2 weeks of the closed season, we went back and built a blind that we could put the boat in, and when the second split opened, we really made some good hunts.

On quite a number of mornings, we were back at my house with our limit of green heads before my children left for school. They would leave home at 8:15 as we lived only 1 block from school.

We did good that season, but the "word" soon spread, and the next season there was too much of a crowd. Most of the duck hunters did not know much about duck hunting and would keep the ducks scared away. This was in 1954 and I have pictures of the hunts.

The author with a limit of "back yard mallards"

"JELLY BEAN" HUNT

To entertain some of our clients, we would schedule hunts and I will tell you about the duck hunts later in this book, however, this was a quail hunt. It was at a facility in Mississippi. As I recall, the name of the facility was Long Leaf Plantation. They had a hunting lodge there that was really, really fine, staffed with some guides. This was a canned hunt I'll call it because the quail that you were going to hunt were pen raised birds but every once in a while you would get into a wild covey.

At this facility, it was strictly first class, we went just as a business entertainment. We would drive up there in two cars, and I guess I need to say here who we brought. I had arranged the hunt for four people- one of the vice presidents in charge of purchasing brought a purchasing agent from a refinery from Lake Charles, and I brought a general manager from a refinery down river from Baton Rouge, right now I don't recall any of the people's name, but it doesn't matter, I'll just go on with what we did. I picked up my client at about 3:00 in the afternoon and it was about three hour drive to Mississippi, not very far north of the Louisiana border, but I don't recall the name of the town. Anyway, my purchasing agent (vice president in charge of purchasing) picked up his client in Lake Charles and we were going to rendezvous at this facility at Long Leaf Plantation.

It was very near dark when we arrived. At this place, they do everything for you, which is not my style, but as I've mentioned before, you have to do that once in a while. You drive up to the lodge and get out of your car and everything is handled for you. All you have to bring is your gun, if you want to. They have guns there for people who do not own a gun, but we brought our own guns and the clients also had guns.

When you get there, you get out of your car and walk into the lodge. Your personal clothing and other gear is then carried to your room and each person has a separate room, a nice facility. This facility is located on the bank of a babbling brook I'll call it.

On the porch or verandah, there are those high back rocking chairs. You overlook this brook and the sound that the water makes is real pleasing.

When we got there, it was near sundown or there about. We went into the lodge and there was a tremendous fireplace with sofas, armchairs, rockers and a fire was roaring in the fireplace. There was a a self service bar, about 15 feet long with every imaginable type of beverage that you could want, with pecans and mixed nuts in dishes along with pretzels, just anything that you wanted in the line of a beverage or refreshing drink. The facility would accommodate eight people, eight hunters. They had two tables with four chairs at each table. After a snack and a drink, you would be offered a choice of several entrees on the menu for that night's dinner, fried quail or baked fish, plus desserts. So, after a good dinner , we would sit around and talk to some of the people that arrived to make up the other foursome. Then we sat down and had a little friendly game of cards. And about 10 o'clock or so everybody turned in. When you got in your room, the attendants had turned down your bed covers, nice down comforters which made a really, really nice place to sleep. From your bedroom, you could hear this brook flowing by the lodge.

The next morning at sunrise, there was a knock on the door and someone called out, "Gentlemen, it's time to get started". We got up and had a fine breakfast, anything you wanted, scrambled eggs, bacon, grits, cereal, coffee, tea, just anything, rolls, donuts, and after a hearty breakfast, we went just out of the lodge where they had a trap arrangement set up where you could shoot a couple of rounds of trap, that's before you went on your quail hunt to get your coordination in effect. So we did that and after that, each two hunters were assigned to a guide. Your transportation was what I call a safari type jeep, that with the high seat on the back and a dog cage on the back with a brace of bird dogs in it. Then we drove a short distance 3 or 4 miles to where we were going to enter the quail runs, I call them. I was informed they had eleven runs, in other words, there were eleven different trails you could take with the feed stations along the way, where the birds had been planted. Now, these birds, the most of them, were pretty good flyers. They would put them out in these locations and they had different types of feed and seed growing there in plots. They would put the birds out and they would fly and run and whatever, but they would stay in that vicinity because of the feed. So, when we approached the first feed plot, the guide released two dogs and they began to work back and forth and the guide driving the jeep would crawl along in low gear and we would sit up on top of the seats there observing the beautiful dog work. Eventually, we would come to a covey and the dogs would point. One dog backing the other, I was familiar with that because my first love like I'd said previously was quail hunting. But with pen raised birds, it's no hurry to get out real quick and run over there to shoot, dismount from the Jeep, get your guns out of the gun box, they had a gun box on the Jeep, load it, put a few extra shells in your jacket pocket and walk over to the pointed dogs with the guide. The guides would flush the birds and the hunters would shoot and the dogs would retrieve what you'd killed. Now some of the birds would fly on, you wouldn't kill them all, usually the coveys were small 7 or 8 birds, but the guide would mark where the other birds lit and we'd go shoot the singles. They wanted you to harvest all the birds because they could not survive in the wild. On most covey rises with the rare exception, we'd end up harvesting the 6 or 7 or 8 quail. Back to the Jeep and ride another 1/4 of a mile to near another feed plot, then we'd repeat the scenario. Well we hunted that morning, back to the lodge for a nice lunch and take a nap if you so desired. There was a nice pond in front of the lodge and we were told this in advance and we did bring a rod and reel or two along and go out and catch a few bass I was lucky enough to catch a couple that were well over four pounds, but released them back into the pond because we were there for hunting and not fishing. Well that afternoon we did the same thing, we switched partners. I took my purchasing agent's client and he took my plant general manager and for the camaraderie, we switched partners. We made another hunt on another run that afternoon and had pretty good luck, too. Then it was another night's lodging at the lodge, another night to sleep and another fine dinner, just as the one before with the real fine wines and really tasty desserts. They had one dessert that stuck in my mind because I love desserts. I want to add before I forget it, this hunting lodge was on a pecan orchard, tremendous orchard, they shipped pecans everywhere. So one of their dishes was chocolate pie with the shell made from crushed pecans and it was really delicious. It may have been near to what they call "Mississippi Mud" which is another chocolate dessert, but it might have had a little variation, but it was really good.

So, with the first morning's hunt and the afternoon hunt complete, we hunted again the next morning. At the end of the hunt which was about 11 o'clock, we went back to the lodge for a snack. The quail that we had harvested were blast frozen and each person was given a little thermos-insulated carrying case with the quail in it. The four of us had bagged 220 quail, so we had 55 quail apiece, 5 quail in each little plastic container, and the containers into each person's insulated bag.

Then all that was left for us to do was to pack up for the journey home. There was a souvenir shop, of course, and we bought souvenirs for our clients to bring home -they picked out what they wanted - maybe a cap or whatever- a memento of Long Leaf Plantation. In fact, that was a lot of years ago, I'm going to say that was in the mid 70's to late 70's. I still have the blaze orange cap that I got for my souvenir from Long Leaf Plantation.

I might add, this is quite expensive, very expensive, I should say and in my case it, could have only been done with corporate dollars, but it paid off in the long run and the president of the company encouraged it. We got to go as one of our perks for being involved with the management of the company. So that was what I call a "jelly bean hunt".

A REAL GOOD OUTING

The weather is pretty outside - kinda cold - it's reading 32° on the thermometer here in Baton Rouge. I guess my boat ride to the camp is going to be a little chilly, but it doesn't take me very long to get there - about 15 minutes- even though it's about 10 miles by water. I'll just bundle up and hurry on down there, go inside the camp, build a fire, then thaw out a little.

Well, I'm at the camp, got here okay. My friend, Raoul Senaca, stopped in. I saw him at the landing and told him to come by the camp and we would make a pot of coffee and he could warm up a little bit. And, lo and behold, he made it, and he is here now. We talked a while, and he left to go to his camp, farther up the channel.

Just as he left, here comes two of my friends from across the canal. Old "Bun" Allen and "Ron" Lawson. "Ron" brought me a sweet potato pie that his wife baked. Boy, that is going to be fine. I'll have a piece of that with my supper. I believe I'm going to have to give him a cooking or two of ducks.

I thought I'd have company tonight, but "Bun" and "Ron" have been out here since Monday and have got to go "to the house" now and freshen up a bit. They won't be there long - before you know it, they will be back, so I guess they will be leaving pretty quick.

Well, this afternoon, the weather moderated a little so I decided to go to the canal and try to catch a bass for supper, and sure enough, I caught two nice bass, one about a pound and a half and one about two pounds, maybe a little better. I filleted them, put them on ice and went to the cove to check on the ducks. There were some ducks there so I hauled some brush and brushed the blind.

I got back to the camp and got ready to fry some fish, peeled a potato and am waiting for the grease to get hot.

I'm the only one "on the hill" tonight. I can't understand that. Here it is in the middle of the hunting season - squirrels, rabbits, ducks, deer and fishing - everything is open season and I'm the "Mayor" out here. No one else is out - nice and peaceful.

It's five minutes to five, I'll be watching the news in a few minutes. By the way, I forgot the corn meal again, so I'll have to go with cracker crumbs again, but I believe my fish supper will come out o.k.

Well I just finished supper, had fish, French fries and sweet potato pie - that was real good. I'm going to watch TV for a while, do a little hygiene - a sponge bath - brush my teeth and go to bed. It's 70° in the house right now, and outside, it's near 30°! I think the weatherman said it is going to get into the 20's tonight, but that doesn't bother me. I've got a good sleeping bag and it's nice and also, it's nice and comfortable in here - got a lot of firewood.

I set the clock for a quarter to four in the morning. I saw enough ducks today on my scouting trip to the cove to make me go out in the morning. I'll try to get my limit. Maybe I will and if I do, that will be great.

I'm going to be here awhile, sitting by the fire, waiting for it to die down, because it's too hot to go to bed right now.

Well, I had a good night's sleep, and I got up as planned. During the night, the weather changed. This morning, it is cloudy and the wind is blowing pretty hard. I heard a little sleet hitting on the tin roof. I hope the wind doesn't get much harder or I'll have trouble paddling my pirogue across the lake to where my blind is located.

I cranked up my boat and cross the canal to start my 20 minute walk through the woods to where my pirogue is stashed and made the walk o.k. The wind didn't increase and the ½ mile paddle was o.k.

I was in my blind 30 minutes before shooting time and had a chance to listen to the sounds of the swamp. Pretty soon, it was time to shoot and the ducks were really flying - that change in the weather really stirred them up. I had my four green heads in about 45 minutes and was paddling out.

This afternoon, about 5:00 p.m., here comes Guy Allen, and his son, Matthew. When they walked up my gang plank and saw those ducks hanging on my porch, their faces lit up with big smiles. Guy said, "Boy, you really had a good hunt". I explained that there were plenty of ducks using by their blind also, so that really got them excited in anticipation of their upcoming hunt.

The next morning, the three of us took off and headed for the blinds. Guy and Mathew hunted together and, as usual, I hunted alone. By 9:00 a.m., we had all limited out and were heading to the camp. Guy and "Matt" were going to stay another day, but I had to go in as I had my two day limit of fat green heads. I would make a few friends in town very happy, but it wouldn't be long before I'd be back. It was a good outing.

A limit of Sawyer's Cove mallards bagged by the author.

ANOTHER HUNT AT THE MOUTH OF THE MISSISSIPPI RIVER

Two of my co-workers and I decided to make a duck hunt below Venice, LA, in the marshes of the Mississippi Delta. This was in the late '50's.

One of the fellows, "Gautreaux", had a 16' aluminum runabout with a 35 HP motor on it, and the other fellow had a 10' x 10' tent with a sewn in bottom and a zipper door. We needed this tent as we intended to spend the night.

We left Baton Rouge early one morning with all our camping gear and supplies for the overnight excursion. We had sleeping bags, a camp stove, and drinking water, plus decoys, guns, lanterns and extra clothing.

We launched our boat at Venice about mid-morning as we had left Baton Rouge early in anticipation of the long drive.

We preceded down river and decided to stop at the coast guard station to check on the area that was open to duck hunting. A lot of that area is set aside as a game refuge, so just to be on the "safe side", we decided to check.

As we approached the station, we saw a helicopter take off and head back towards New Orleans - we didn't think too much of it at the time, but marveled at the ducks that took to the air when the helicopter flew over them.

We went inside and was waiting to see the attendant in charge when we saw a wet tennis shoe on the floor. When the attendant came out, he directed us to a huge map on the wall that was color coded with the off limit areas, making it clear as to where we could hunt. He cautioned us about cotton mouth water moccasins, as a hunter had just been bitten and the helicopter had airlifted him from the station en route to a New Orleans hospital.

We proceeded down river and picked out a spot where we could drag the boat upon shore, as the river traffic is quite heavy and you cannot leave your boat in the water due to the wave action.

As soon as we got on shore, we spotted 2 cottonmouths. It had been warm and the sudden cold front caught them out of their den and they were real sluggish. If we had not had a tent with a bottom and zipper door, we would not have slept there.

That evening, we had a good hunt - mostly widgeons and teal - and when it got dark, we did not venture out of the tent, remembering that wet tennis shoe and the 2 snakes that had greeted us earlier that day.

After supper, we went to bed and had a good night's sleep. The next morning, we waited until good daylight arrived before we ventured out for our hunt.

As we had no blind, we hunted along side of a fence that went out into the marsh. The grass had grown up besides the fence and we had good cover from one side. We put the decoys on the other side.

We saw several more snakes that morning and they were all lethargic from the cold weather and would not get out of our paths. They would just open that big mouth and you could quickly tell why they are called, "cotton mouths".

Despite being very cautious, we had a good hunt - we came back with our two day limit.

HIGH WATER DUCK HUNTING

As anyone knows who hunts ducks, high water is bad news especially early in the season when the ducks are scattered out so much. When this happens in the Atchafalaya Basin, I have a method of hunting.

I would put my pirogue in my bateau and proceed up one of the canals that lead from the levee to the middle of the swamp. The only land above water is the spoil bank deposited by the dredge when they cut the canal. I would pick a straight section of the canal and park my bateau on the opposite side from the side that I was going to hunt. Like that when you came out, if you were not at exactly the right spot, you can see your boat better. I would arrive at the place I wanted to hunt before daylight with my gun, shells, compass, two paddles, plus lunch and water, I would start out.

Now you have to understand you are paddling in a flooded woodland, no land and at times thick underbrush, You paddle as quietly as you can because your only chance for a successful hunt is to get close enough for jump shooting.

I put my compass on the floor of the pirogue and try to maintain a general direction so, when it's time to head back, I won't miss my bateau by too much. This is usually an all day hunt. I stop about noon and break out the Vienna sausage and crackers. I try to find a big log to pull up to as to steady the pirogue where I can stand and stretch my legs. I start back to my boat well before dark whether I have any luck or not. Even though I am not afraid of getting lost, it is difficult to paddle through that heavy brush at night. Sometimes, I would do pretty good, other times not, but it was one way to try to make a hunt.

High water mallards bagged by the author, paddling the swamp

WADING - ANOTHER MEANS OF TAKING DUCKS

This technique of hunting - wading - is a little different from "blind hunting". I'd like to discuss some of my experiences about wading.

You need to go down to a sporting goods store and buy a pair of chest high waders and also a pair of oversized tennis shoes. In other words, I wear size 10 boots and I buy size 12 tennis shoes and it needs to be the ones with the high tops so that you can lace them up real tight. You do not want any low quarters, they have got to be high tops. Then you will need to purchase a pair of suspenders if the waders that you purchased didn't come with suspenders.

My first encounter with wading for ducks in flooded woods was in a lake near Atchafalaya River, Lost Lake was the name. A commercial fisherman had a camp there that my father-in-law had access to as they were friends. We would launch our boat at Butte LaRose and it was about a three mile journey up river to Mr. Melancon's camp where we would spend a night. The next morning it was about 1/4 of a mile walk from the camp on a path to the edge of the water. We would walk that short distance with our regular leather boots or rubber boots on and when we got to the edge of the water we would take off those boots and put on the waders and tennis shoes. Doing that type of hunting you need to be particular about your hunting coat because if you didn't put it inside your waders, you had a good possibility of getting your shells or whatever you had in your coat wet.

We had to wade out to where the trees were kind of sparse because if you didn't you wouldn't have an opening through which to shoot. But we would wade out almost waist deep, or waist deep in places, to try to find an opening between the trees where you could shoot if ducks would fly. You always had a good bottom to walk on, it was fun, there weren't any muddy bottoms because you were actually hunting in the high water section of the lake. That would be in late December, early January, when the river would rise and it would raise the level of the lake and it would put water over land that had been dry most of the year all through the summer months. So you had good footing. All you needed was a duck call. You didn't have to have any decoys, wade out and try to find an opening in the trees where you could shoot through. That would be sufficient to do that kind of hunt. You want to get in a spot where you can have an opening above you and be real particular of where you stood because most of your shots were nearly straight up. It would be very easy to shoot and get kicked back and fall in the water, so I would try to get against a substantial brush or small tree, put your back against that support because when you did get recoil from your gun and you were shooting nearly straight up, and standing in water waist deep, you could not catch your balance very easily. You'll learn after a few mishaps that you need to do that. The only other thing you'd do besides call would be to take your foot and move it back and forth and make ripples on the water and that worked real well and they would come over treetop high. You can usually get your ducks, and when they were really decoying good, they would come down through the trees. Boy, that was really some fine shooting! One time, three of us were hunting there, we were lucky enough to get our 12 mallards, 4 a piece that day. We spent a night and the next morning we limited out again, we had 24 fine mallards and that was a good hunt.

    We got to hunt there several more times and most of the time we would have a decent hunt, sometimes better than others. We finished out the duck season hunting in that particular place by wading. We did good that year.

    The next time I had the occasion to hunt wading was in the 70's. That's a long span from the time we hunted in that section. I was doing a job at Dow Chemical and I made the acquaintance of some hunters and they knew of a place in the Bayou Sorrel area off of a little bayou named Bayou Indigo. These fellows had gotten some news that the ducks were using in that area. So we spent a night at a camp that they had access to. The next morning before daylight, we got in the boat and went several miles to the mouth of Indigo Bayou. There was a log jam in that bayou and we had to leave our boat there and walk the rest of the way. We didn't have the luxury of walking there in leather boots or short knee boots, we had to leave the camp with our waders on, tennis shoes, headlights and flashlights and make the trip by walking along the banks of Indigo Bayou. The person who had alerted us to ducks in that area couldn't give us specific directions on how to get to them. He just said walk down Indigo Bayou about mile and then cut in towards the woods and the flooded woodland.

So, sure enough, we did that and as luck would have it we were walking and one of the fellows had to stop and relieve himself. We all stopped and we couldn't have stopped in a better place because it was about 15 or 20 minutes before daylight and off to the west, we were walking south at the time, we could hear the mallard ducks calling. They do that a lot of time in the early morning just before they take off to feed and what not. We said, "Here we are- we're in the right spot." We spread out maybe 50 or 75 yards apart and walked into the woods until we hit the edge of the water and then out into the water until about waist deep. We took up a stand and sure enough the ducks were really in that area. We each had a call and we were calling and making ripples in the water and those ducks really came in. We made a fantastic hunt. We had the limit and we came out and everybody wanted to go back the next morning. I told those fellows, "We shot them pretty good this morning, I don't know if they are going to be here tomorrow." "Oh yes", they said, "they are going to be here. With all those ducks they are bound to be here".

We spent another night at the camp and in the meantime we were joined by another hunter. As luck would have it, the next morning and the four of us killed a total of five ducks. The ducks did move -they do that when you put pressure on them. That was the last time I hunted in that area.

The next time I hunted ducks wading was in Sawyer's Cove in the 80's- probably '82 or '83. The water came up high early in the season. Where we had our blind situated, there just wasn't any use to try to get a duck to come in there. We noticed that the ducks were going into the flooded woods. We tried at first with pirogues and it was really too dense to maneuver a pirogue in there, too many down logs, so we said we'll see if we can make it with hip boots. Water was to deep for hip boots, you couldn't do it. So it was back to town buying waders and tennis shoes again and back to the cove. And sure enough we made it. It was the same setup, you'd get in the water, no decoys, just your caller. Call and make the ripples if you can and they'd come in and you make your hunt. We were able to hunt in that part several times to round out the season.

That was about the last time I can remember hunting with waders other than hip boots. But I still keep a pair of waders at my camp and a pair of tennis shoes. I have them stored, if the need arises I've got the equipment there to do it. It is a good way to hunt but a little cold, when you're in that water, it gets a little cold if the weather is inclimate, but if that's the way they want it, that's the way you've got to give it to them.

Wading paid off for the author - a limit of green heads!

Chest high waders & tennis shoes with push pole.

SOUNDS FROM A DUCK BLIND

I've touched on this earlier, but this past season was the first time that I brought my tape recorder in the duck blind. I've taken a camera many times, but this particular morning, I decided to bring the recorder.

On this morning, I saw the greatest concentration of mallards I've ever seen and they were coming in at daylight by the hundreds. I've been hunting ducks for 50 plus years and I have never seen a spectacle like this. They were literally lighting all around me- the sound that they were making on the water was something to hear. Hundreds of ducks at a time coming over me, silhouetted against the sky. I'm an old duck hunter but I sat there in disbelief as they continued to pour in. My tape recorder records my exclamation in my voice saying that I wish every duck hunter would have this opportunity to see this spectacle one time.

I could have had my limit in the first 10 minutes if I had so desired, but I would not shoot until most of this fantastic sight was over. By then, I started to call and in a short period of time, I had my four green heads. I was paddling out after 30 minutes of legal shooting time.

A RICE FIELD DUCK HUNT

One Friday evening, my family and I arrived at my "inlaws" farm,and as usual, I had my equipment with me as we usually made a duck hunt in the swamp above Henderson, LA.

It had been raining all day and was still raining when we arrived. After unloading the car, George, my father-in-law, started making plans for a hunt. He said, "Bud, we will never make it to the camp as that levee will be impassable. I have written previously about going by horseback to the camp after a rain.

Not wanting to disappoint me, he came up with another plan. He said that an acquaintance of his owned some rice field acreage west of Lafayette, LA, at Duson, and he was told he could hunt there if he desired. I told him let's try it, but I thought we'd be real lucky if we had any success.

I had brought my waders as I had intended to wade the back water in the swamp above Henderson, but the decoys were at the camp, so George said we would have to do the best we could.

We set the clock for 3:00 a.m. and after arising, proceeded to Duson. We turned north off of the highway and came to the field that we were to hunt. It was still raining when we arrived which was perfect weather for the rice field hunt. We donned our waders and rain parkas and crossed the fence into the rice field. It was still 30 minutes before shooting time.

We walked about 200 yards off the road to get away from the truck. There was a couple of inches of water on a knoll and that's where we decided to hunt. With our waders on, we were able to sit on the ground!

When shooting time came, it was still heavily overcast and as the ducks started to fly, we began to call, and bagged several mallards.

It then got light and the ducks could see us and would not come in. I told George that we had to move. We had four ducks at that time.

About 100 yards away, there was the corner of a barbed wire fence, so we went to that spot and hung rice straw on the barbed wire. We made a partial blind by placing our 4 dead ducks out as decoys, sticking reeds in the mud and putting their bills over the reeds. It looked like they were feeding.

It did not take very long before we had four more mallards for our limit. I was really surprised that we succeeded that well. This just proves that you must go out and give it your best shot -no matter what the conditions.

Two limits of mallards on an improvised hunt in a rice field.

FIRST QUAIL HUNTING TRIP

My dad was a bird hunter, quail and dove, and occasionally he'd make a squirrel hunt or a rabbit hunt with some of his friends, but bird hunting was the big thing, quail. He always had a bird dog. When I was 12 years old or so, my dad starting taking me bird hunting with him. I learned to hunt with a double barrel 410. We had a dog, liver and white pointer, Bill was his name. We went with old Bill, went up north of Baton Rouge up around Scotlandville, and there was a lot of open land. In fact, the old cemetery is still there and my dad used to hunt across from what they call the Maryland Tank Farm, that was out in the country. Also we'd go out on Anselmo Lane, pretty close to where one of TV stations is now. And we'd hunt on Mr. Anselmo's property,. And we'd hunt quail, and I remember the very first time I'd killed a quail over a pointed dog. We had a covey rise and my dad got two or three - he always did, and lo and behold, I swung on a pair and I got one, to make matters better, old Bill went and retrieved it for me and that was a real thrill.

JELLY BEAN HUNT #2

Being a member of management at Jacobs Construction Company, I was allowed to schedule duck hunts in the marshes of southwest Louisiana for our clients.

About twice a year, once during the 1st split and then again during the second split, I would arrange a hunt.

In preparation for the hunt, I would send out for the supplies we would need to the local sporting goods store. The list included shotgun shells of various gauges, mosquito repellent, camouflaged caps, gloves and so forth. Also, we would send out to the local stores for cold drinks, beer, snack foods, etc., all being done after confirming a hunting date at the duck camp.

Several times we went to the Pintail Club at Pecan Island. This establishment was run by Mr. Dyson. His place accommodated 12 hunters. His staff included an elderly couple who handled the cooking chores.

There were several large rooms with a number of clean beds to sleep in, as well as a large eating area, kitchen and bath facilities. It was a kind of rustic atmosphere, but it served the purpose.

We would leave Baton Rouge about mid-morning to make the 3 hour trip to the marsh. We would have 3 cars with 4 people in each car. On some of the trips, I would take my "labor relations" person or a "vice president in charge of sales" or possibly a "superintendent" from one of the larger jobs, and they would also invite a guest.

We would arrive at the camp in time to make an afternoon hunt, spend the night, then hunt again the next morning.

There was a guide for every 2 hunters, and he would have a retriever. We would be transported to the marsh in a truck or van, then into a mud boat for the ride to the blinds.

I always hunted with the head guide and I would tell him to instruct the other guides to let the clients do the shooting. If you didn't give these instructions, the guides would kill all the ducks. The guides did resent this, however, as they wanted to shoot.

After the afternoon hunt, it was back to the lodge for supper which was always good. They usually prepared duck for supper, along with gravy, biscuits and some vegetables. Then, it was time to go to bed for a little rest before the morning hunt.

We would be awakened very early so that we could eat breakfast and have time to make the trip back out to the blinds as we had done the previous afternoon.

After a light breakfast of coffee, rolls, doughnuts or cereal and milk, it was off to the hunt. The mud boat was quite large with a big V-8 motor in it. The head guide would drop off 2 hunters and a guide at each blind, then leave me and my client at the last blind, hide the mud boat, and come back to us in his pirogue.

After about 9 a.m., the hunt was over and we would pick up every one and go back to the lodge. On the way back, we would drop off the ducks at a place that picked and wrapped the ducks for us to bring home. They charged $0.75 a piece to clean the birds.

Once back at the lodge, it was time for the "real" breakfast - bacon, eggs, grits, deer sausage, biscuits, milk, juice, coffee - and most anything else you may want.

After breakfast, we would wait for the ducks that were being cleaned and then get ready to return home. I would sign the bill, tip the guides and, I must add, the price was quite expensive. But, it was good for business and that was a perk for us being in management. Last came the journey home with a few ducks and a lot of good memories.

"RUSTY"

A retriever is a very valuable asset for a duck hunter. It will definitely cut down on lost cripples. I had a chocolate lab that I acquired at two months old. I trained him myself. Rusty was his name, and he was quite a dog. It never got too tough for Rusty. I hunted the marsh one season in the 70's when the point system was in effect and you could legally bag 10 ducks if you were selective in what species you bagged. My partner and I bagged several hundred ducks that season without losing any. Rusty lived to be 16 years old. I didn't take him out his last three years, but when I had to have him "put down", it was a sad day. He's buried in my backyard now with a marker by his grave. I lost a good devoted friend when I lost Rusty. His picture is on my den wall. If you have the facilities for a dog, get a retriever. They make good pets and are good hunting companions. It is not to difficult to train one.

I've talked quite a lot about my dog, Rusty. When I get started, I can't stop. I'll really bend your ear. Rusty had a great ability to mark falls of ducks by the sounds and you didn't have to give him a line or hand signal him either. I've seen him mark two ducks when one fell on one side of the blind and one on the other. This was in the marsh when we had a pirogue pulled up on a little island. When the ducks fell, he went to the right and brought that duck back, dropped it in the pirogue and out the other side to get the second duck without a sign or hand signal or sound from me. I've seen Rusty go to the shore with a big duck in his mouth to do a "big job" or a "little job" and never put the duck down, then bring it on in. He was quite a dog.

I need to add something humorous about Rusty. Mr. Mack and I were in a blind one morning and Rusty was between us. Things got kind of slow, so I broke out the bite size candy bars that I keep in hunting jacket pocket, usually six pieces, one piece for Mack, one for Rusty and one for me. I peeled Rusty's piece and with one gulp, it was gone. About 30 minutes later, another candy break and the same scenario. Just as I started to eat my candy, a flight of ducks appeared on the horizon and we stooped down in the blind to see if they would come close enough to call. While stooping down, Rusty decided to lick my candy bar, so that time he got two pieces of candy and I got none, We had a good laugh about that.

"Rusty" at 16 months old.

My dog, "Rusty".

The author pulling a pirogue in the swamp.

"DAN"

I've had English Setters, Liver and White, Lemon and White, Black and White Pointers. I've written something about Dan earlier in this book, but I need to add something else. Dan was really the best bird dog I've ever owned.

I got Dan when he was a young dog, partially trained, but because his owner was going into field trial dogs and Dan was a bird hunter's dog, I got him. I used to tell my friends that Dan could "make" a covey of quail, that's how good he was. When he hit a field, all you had to do was stay on the head land and he would quarter that field and with a wave of my arm, it was to the next section of the field. He had the uncanny ability to stop a covey from running on the ground. If they would not hold, he would not creep and follow like a lot of dogs do, he would break point, make a half circle and point them from the other side. They would have to run over him if they wanted to run. He hardly ever flushed, as he knew how close to get. After the covey would rise, we would go to get the singles.

I've seen Dan, on several occasions, be retrieving a dead bird and on the way in, point another bird with a dead bird in his mouth. Dan was a fantastic bird dog, but I lost him in his prime, about eight years old. He died of heart worms. At that time, which was in the 50's, they didn't have a cure. I lost a good dog and I also mentioned that I had not raised Dan from a puppy, but he had not bonded to his previous owner as he had a trainer. So when I got him, he became my dog.

You know the affection that your dog shows when he sees you, his eyes bright and alert, his mouth happy and appearing to smile and his eagerness to lick your hand for a pat on the head. Your dog will be completely devoted to you and will do anything for you that you can convey for him to do.

OBEYING HUNTING RULES AND REGULATIONS

The next thing I want to talk about is hunting rules and regulations. Always obey the state and federal hunting regulations.

As a duck hunter, I know how difficult it is to stop shooting when you get your limit when there are hundred of ducks in the air and you have only been in the blind for 30 minutes or so. One of my friends once said, "...it is better to hunt like a game agent is in the blind with you..." and those are true words.

We do have a liberal season now and a good limit, which is because of conservation. I can remember in the early 60's of a 19-day duck season and a one mallard limit. One mallard daily limit, two possession limit. We certainly don't want those restrictions to be placed on us again. So, obey the game laws, you will come out ahead in the end.

A fine pair of mallards.

Ducks in the morning.

Bass in the afternoon.

FISHING

FISHIN' HOLES AROUND

I have fished many places in Louisiana. I'd like to write about some of these places.

<u>Ox Bow Lakes</u>

"False River", which I have mentioned earlier, was formed when the Mississippi River changed its course by cutting across a bend to take a shorter route. "False River" is located at New Roads, LA, which is approximately 40 miles west of Baton Rouge. I first fished there in the 30's. It is still a good place to fish, but now, a shadow of what it was many years ago.

"Old River" is an ox bow lake near Morganza, LA. It is heavily fished even today. The largest bass I ever caught, 7 pounds, 8 ½ ounces, was caught there, in 1959.

Lake Concordia, located in Ferriday, LA, is further up the Mississippi.

Lake Bruin (located at St. Joseph), Lake St. John, near Clayton, LA, and Lake Providence, at the town of the same name are also great fishing spots and also good pleasure boat lakes.

<u>Barrow Pits:</u>

There are numerous Barrow Pits along the Mississippi River as well as the Atchafalaya River. These pits were formed when the Corps of Engineers excavated dirt from an area to either build or reinforce the levee structures. Thus the name, "barrow pit" was coined. Some of the pits are still very good for fishing, but many have been drained as it was discovered that the pits were allowing the levees to remain saturated too long. Further, the adjoining landowners still maintain the ownership rights to the land therefore, that land can be legally posted by the landowner. (The government only paid for the easement rights).

The author's sons holding a 7 lb., 8.5 oz. bass caught in Old River above Morganza, LA.

As for bayous, streams, canals, bays and other impoundments, such as ponds, they number literally thousands, and thus, too numerous to name, but here are a few:

Bayou Courtableau	Miller's Lake
Ramah Pits	Grassy Lake
Sunk Lake	Bayou Des Ourse
BigAlabama	Little Alabama
Bayou Sorrel	Grand River Flats
Bayou Pigeon	Grand Lake
Avoca Island Lake	Lake Pension
Lake Decade	Amarada Canal
Philips Canal	Berry Lake
Spikes Bay	Grand Bay
Sawyer's Cove	Lake Henderson
Fish Bayou Lake	Belson Lake
Cow Island Lake	Lost Lake
LakeVerret	Sugar Mill Chute
Belle River	Lake Palourde
Pat's Bay	

All of these I have fished, and I can name dozens more.

MY FIRST FISHING TRIP

I can recall the first time that my dad took me fishing. It was on City Park Lake, if you can imagine that. Someone had told him if you go down there and rent a boat, which you could at that time, and paddle it across the lake and pull your boat across a little old gravel road, a little body of water is there and there are some bass in it. Sure enough, I was maybe five years old. I don't remember pulling it across, but it is vivid in my mind that he caught one of the bass and I have the recollection of the bass, my dad with the fish, its mouth open and it was caught on a yellow bucktail shimmy wiggler, at the time that was one of the favorite baits. I do remember he caught three bass. Now that is the earliest that I can recall a fishing trip.

When I was nine or ten years old, I got a hand-me-down casting rod and reel. The rod, if I remember right was a tubular steel rod. At that time they had tubular steel and solid steel. There weren't any fiberglass rods or anything like that. I guess some people had real expensive bamboo rods, but that was an exception. I learned to cast with a bunch of store string on the reel and a nut or bolt tied on it. I would be in the yard throwing it trying to hit a target, and not having much luck, but trying to get proficient enough to go fishing. So, as time went by, I guess when I was around 12 years old, I got the chance to go fishing with my dad. He worked six days a week, off on Sunday, and Sunday was a church day, of course. So most of the time, if we went fishing, it was after church. That was kind of a late start, even though at one time they had a Fisherman's Mass at St. Joseph's Cathedral. The fishermen would show up in their fishing clothes. I think the Mass was 4:00 a.m.. Then you would catch the ferry, because there weren't any bridges then. It took you across to the river, to False River, Ramah, and places to the west, because on this side of the river, which is the east side of the Mississippi River at Baton Rouge, there is a lot of tide action which affects the fishing, and most anytime you went on this side of the river, the tide was either in too high or going out to fast or whatever. But I went with him several times and never did have any luck, he might catch one or two, but I didn't catch any. I had a little tackle box three or four lures in it. Someone told me I should go down to Montgomery Ward, which was on Third Street and buy a shimmy wiggler. At that time shimmy wiggler, shannon spinner, lucky 13 and that was the lures. I had saved up a few coins, I had 89 cents, if I remember. We lived on 20th Street and Montgomery Ward was on 3rd Street, so I talked somebody into walking with me, one of the neighborhood kids. We walked to 3rd Street and went into Montgomery Ward and asked the clerk if we could see a shimmy wiggler and sure enough he got out some. I said I would like to have this one with the yellow tail on it, he said it was 98 cents. Well, I didn't have but 89 cents, so I said, "Well, I guess I'll have to come back in a week or two when I can save up a little bit more and get it". That was no big deal, I walked home. I didn't get to buy the lure. Well, my dad had a friend that worked at Standard Oil, you know that is Exxon now. The man was Mr. Dalton Hanks. He came by one day, he was a big fisherman. He was really successful at catching bass and he loved to fish False River, so he said, "Rock" (that was my daddy's name) "let me take that boy fishing, I believe I can make him catch a fish". My dad said, " that will be fine with me if he wants to go". I said "Yes sir, I'd be happy to go". He said, " I tell you what, I'll pick you up Saturday morning at around 3:30, we got to catch the 4:00 ferry, because we got to get over to False River early". There is a man on the lower end of False River had three or four old skiffs that he would rent you. But you'd better get there early or you would not get one. The skiffs were rented to you for 50 cents. And if he didn't have anything to do, he'd paddle you all day for a dollar. So sure enough, I set the clock, my mama made sure I got up and along come Mr. Dalton Hanks, I'll never forget him. Model-A Ford, I guess about a '29 model, before they started making anything better and away we went. Caught the ferry and journeyed to False River, that was a long journey, probably 35 miles. And when we got there, sure enough this old fellow that rented the boats didn't have anything to do. And Mr. Hanks said, (I believe the man's name was Mr. Bush). . "Mr. Bush, would you like to paddle for us today?" Mr. Bush said, "why sure, I'd be glad to, well let's go." Sure enough, we got in one of those 16 feet cypress skiffs. You know at that time we are talking about 1935 maybe 1936, not very many people had a motor- there weren't any on False River. So we got in the boat, starting fishing, I had my little lures on- casting away. Mr. Dalton had gone to H & W Hardware on Main Street. They had some plugs there, they call them crank bait now. They were 25 cents a piece. They were made out of wood and had a couple of sets of treble hooks on them and a metal bill in front that would make it dive down. Of course you had to get them and adjust them to make them swim right. And we starting casting. In fact, I had one, too. We went along there a little piece and, low and behold, Mr. Hanks caught a fish, reeled it in, a nice little bass -couple of pounds. He immediately cut the lure off his line, he said "Here son, tie this lure on your line". I can remember it as if it was yesterday. It was an off colored white plug, crank bait, had a dark green stripe down the back and had silver glitter on it, we used to call that the silver flash. I put the bait on and starting casting, and by dog, I caught a fish. And boy was I thrilled and to make matters better, it weighed 3 lbs.. and 5 oz. We continued to fish and fish from daylight till around 2:00, and we had a total of seven bass. And I had caught 4 and Mr. Dalton had caught 3. Was I ever proud to get home and show the folks that I had finally caught some bass. I never will forget Mr. Dalton Hanks, he's gone now. He was a fine man and I used to enjoy hearing he and my daddy talk about fishing trips. They went a lot together, went to some nice places and caught some good fish, all local of course. But that one time, that really broke the ice and it made me a bass fisherman and I'm still a bass fisherman. My kids don't like to hear me say it, "I'm 75 years old" because I'm stretching a little bit, I'm 74, will be 75 in three months. That was a long time ago, I had to be maybe twelve years old. It was a fine experience, like I said I'll never forget it.

Going along the same lines, after that first encounter catching a bass, I fished pretty regular with my dad, whenever he could find the time to go. We'd go to different places. We had one place we'd go to called Bayou Latenache, it was a nice little stream and then we built a little plywood boat we could carry on top of the car. This was in around I'd say 1937 or 1938. We had a '34 Ford. We had car top racks for it. We could take off and go early but we still had to cross the ferry. I must have been around I guess 13 or 14 years old. We'd go west of Baton Rouge. Went to Bayou Ramah, went to Bayou Courtableau and False River again. We'd go to several places in one day- we'd unload that little boat off the top of the car and put it in the water and go on. We've had some successful trips like that.

A 6 lb. and a 7 lb. bass caught at False River by the author.

OLD FISHING EQUIPMENT AND LURES

Prior to 1930, some of the fishing gear was on the market would now be antique, of course. My dad learned to bait cast with the reels that didn't have a level winder on them. I believe that's the reason even today a lot of people will fish with a rod and reel and they palm the reel, in fact, that's the way I fish. In your left hand, the butt plate or the butt cap of the reel is actually in the palm of your hand. In those days the reason that you had to do that is because the fisherman used his thumb to distribute the line back and forth over the spool. By the time I come along they did have level winders on the reel. In his early days of fishing that was the reel and the rods, I believe exclusively solid steel and short, 3, 3-1/2, very few 4 feet casting rods. And they had the straight handle on them and the cork grip on the handle. True Temper made a solid steel rod and like I said 3-1/2, 4 feet is what the fishermen used. The rods usually have two or maybe three guides. The end guide had an agate tip that was suppose to keep your line from wearing too much. Of course, they would groove or if you would hit one against an object you would break the agate guide and you would have to unsolder that guide, go down and get another one and solder it on. The fishing lures at that time and the line was obsolete according to today's standard. The lines were mostly linen and you would get a 50 yard spool of linen line usually 18 to 20 pound test. When you'd come back from fishing you'd need to string it out in the backyard on a clothes pole and let it dry. If you didn't, it would rot on that spool. Even going through those precautions the next time you went fishing it was a good idea to break off 6 to 8 feet of the end of that line before you tied your lure on. Of course, you know that was long before these nylon lines and monofilament lines and all that new-fangled lines that are out today. In talking about the rod, one of my dad's friends came by one day and he had just purchased a new rod. It was one of the longer ones, I guess it was long as any they had at the time, I guess it was 5 feet long. True Temper supposedly had a reputation that you could take that steel rod and bend a circle in it from tip to butt and it would not break. So when this friend walked by with his new rod, we approached him about that guarantee and he said, "Yes, you can do it." We said, "well, let us see you do it." So, sure enough, he bent the rod in a circle and it practically touched the tip and it didn't break, but when he straightened it out, it had a kind of a kink in it and I believe he was really disgusted. But he said, "Maybe it'll straighten out."

I believe the next rod that they came out with was the Tubular Steel of which I acquired one of those second hand tubular rods and an old reel I had described previously. But it did have a level winder on it. The lures in that period of time were heavy lures. They weighed from 3/4 of an ounce to over an ounce. Some of the top water lures have as many as 15 hooks on them, five sets of treble hooks. I know that lure weighed well over an ounce.

Some of the old fishing lures that were around when I first starting fishing - I guess now, a lot of people do not even know that they existed. But as I've mentioned in some of the other articles I've written previously, one of the favorite lures of the old fisherman was the Shimmy Wiggler. It was made I believe by a company Al Faust. It was a buck tail bait had a kind of spoon disk on it in the front. You had a screw that you could remove and change the buck tail. They had a lot of various colors, I remember a yellow, red and white, red and black, solid white and several varieties. On this lure a lot of times, the thing to do was put a piece of pork rind on the back - we would say we're going to sweeten that bait up a little bit. We would put it on that hook and it would make a nice little flutter back there, that was before the rubber skirts, there weren't any rubber skirts then. That type of lure, if you pulled it rapidly, it would come across the water making a nice little furrow through the water, you would get some real good strikes and you could slow it down and get some strikes under water, too. Most of the fisherman liked to run it fast.

Then another lure about that same era was the Shannon Twin Spinner. It also was a buck tail lure. You could run it on top, but it was more difficult, because it didn't have that scooped out metal in front that would keep it up top. It was a lead head with two wires coming up with about a number one or smaller Colorado or Indiana spinner on it. That too, you could put a piece of pork rind on, but we didn't use pork rind on that one as much. And also that was a very, very good night lure. It came in the various buck tail patterns. You couldn't change the buck tail on that one, it was wrapped on to the lead head of that lure. But it was a good bait for all around fishing, like I said night fishing also.

Another lure that was around about that time was the Lucky 13. The Lucky 13 as you may know is a wooden plug. Of course since then, it has been reproduced in plastic. But everybody agreed that the old wooden plug was the best. It too had three sets of trebles - kind of a large bait, I would say three quarters of an ounce. The way to work that bait was to cast it out in a likely spot, let it set and twitch it a time or two. A lot of times, you'd get a vicious strike on top, but then sometimes they would hit the lure when you started to reel it in and it was a good lure, also. They had a bait called the vamp I think was the name of it and they had the straight model and also the jointed and they had a metal lip on it if you will, it too had several sets of treble hooks. You could work it on top or you could reel it and it also produced good results. There was another wooden lure, the vamp was wood also, I think the name of it was Dowagiac. It had a real odd shape metal bill on it, wooden plug, but it was more or less strictly under water lure, that's way back. Then there was a spinner called the Buel Spinner. It was a straight wire with a tandem spinners on it propeller type spinner, and a buck tail on the back with a treble hook. I think I remember right, it was feathers instead of hair on the tail. It was a good lure. Another lure that was similar to the Shimmy Wiggler I think they called it Dixie Siren, you would work it similar to the Shimmy Wiggler, and it was way back, too.

You had some spoons at that time, too. One of the popular spoons - I think they called it the Dare Devil. It came in a pattern of red and white stripes and there was another one I remember -

black and white stripes. There was one set of treble hooks on the back. The next spoon I'm going to mention is still around, it's an oldie. It was the Johnson Spoon. It had a single hook with a weed guard and that was also a good lure to put a piece of pork rind on. Of course, they had the jointed darter and they made the straight darter also, it was really, really a fine lure.

  As we progressed up into the more recent times, one of the favorite lures was the River Runt, oh if you didn't have a few river runts, to use in a lot of the impoundments we went to, there wasn't any use in going. Then some of the fellows knew how to rig that river runt where it was really more effective than when it came from the factory so they claimed, that was matter of opinion. The River Runt was a small lure with a metal lip it was also a crank bait. It had an eye on the front to tie your line to retrieve it. Some of the fellows would, instead of tying the line in the eye, take a small jeweler's file and cut a notch in the very top of the eye and then they would experiment with various kinds of knots where they could tie the line in that notch. In fact, they called it a notched river runt. Instead of the lure when you retrieve it having a wobble to it, it had a more tight, tight wiggle. In fact, now you have a lot of lures that imitate that same wiggle. The Spot and several others are the Swimming Minnow, let me see if I can think of another one. Another one they called the Sonic and the Rattle Trap. These lures were lipless, crank bait, if you will. They didn't have a lip on them, but by having the eye in the back of the lure on top in front of the dorsal fin, it gave that same quiver that the notched river runt used to give that these fellows claim that they were better than the original way it came from the factory. Of course that's argumentative, some people used it and some didn't. That was always a question for debate.

  Then came, in the early 50's or mid 50's, the Howser Hell Diver, and boy that's started a revolution in fishing as far as I'm concerned. I'm sure from the time the Howser Hell Diver came out, which was a safety pin type of spinner bait, it had a lead head, a wire shaped like a safety pin at the top and it had about a number

2-1/2 or 3 willow leaf spinner. Then they came out with one that had a Colorado spinner on it and it was a heavy lure, it pulled heavy, a lot of people didn't like it because it was pretty heavy reeling. That started a revolution and I would imagine since that Howser Hell Diver came out, there has been hundreds of variations with different types of spinner arrangements, a lot of double spinners with two Colorados or two Indianas or Willow Leaf spinners on the shaft. Some of them had three, one in front of the lead head. It caught thousands and thousands of fish and it will still catch fish. It is still one of the most popular lures in the tackle box, in fact, it is one of my most popular- favorite I should say.

While I'm on the subject of these old lures, I want to relate something to you that concerns one of these lure and that's the Shannon Spinner that I spoke about. I know it was in the 30's or 40's. It had to be in the 30's. In the one of the impoundments that I fished, some of the local plantation workers would get a cane pole, the cane pole would be as long as they could handle without to much difficulty. But I say the cane pole would be 12 or 14 feet long. They would tie a piece of heavy line, not the fishing line as we know it now, but a piece of heavy staging I call it, put a shannon spinner on the end of it and wade out into the water waist deep, now this was in the good summer time. More or less, with that shannon spinner on the end of that rod and line, not in the motion that you would do a fly rod, but they would weave it from side to side as they walked and kind of flip it, if you will, over by a grass bed, no reel just the cane pole about 12 -14 feet long whatever they could handle, line about the same length. They would catch a real nice string of bass. Of course at that time, there weren't too many rod and reels. I've covered some of that before. The rod and reels at that time were primitive. Those fellows who worked and lived on the plantations would go out there with that primitive arrangement and catch a nice mess of fish.

String of hybrid stripper bass ranging from 6 lbs. to 9 lbs. caught at False River by the author.

FISHING TRIPS - NO MOTOR

In '39, I was in high school- Baton Rouge High - on the football team, I was 16 years old, and bought my first hunting and fishing license which I still have and I bought a duck stamp. I wasn't into duck hunting at the time, but my dad said, "You know you'd better buy a stamp just in case you might be out hunting and you might get to shoot at a duck.". Also, I bought a fishing license.

Well, there was a local establishment down about a block from our house - a little tavern. Of course, being on the football team at that time that was a "no no" - anybody going there to drink a beer, but I used to love going down there and they had some of these old bass fishermen who worked at Standard Oil, Exxon again. Mr. Bill Fugler was one, B.C. Wilson, Mr. Ford. This establishment was run by Mr. Giaconne, been knowing him for a long time, and I loved to go down there and listen to the old fellows talk about bass fishing. Occasionally when three of the men were going fishing and they needed somebody to go with them so that there would be two to a boat, they'd invite me to go. You know the gas rationing was on at that time and those fellows used to pool their coupons to buy gas for us to go fishing. Boy, whenever they'd ask me, I was glad to go and they were glad to have me. We started fishing the upper end of False River. There was a Mr. Joe Hilbert who had a camp and I believe it was the only camp on the river side of the highway. I would say today it's over a thousand on that side. But, anyway Mr. Hilbert had four or five cypress skiffs, and he had oar locks on them. You'd rent a skiff for 50 cents, but you'd better be there early. So we'd crossed on the early ferry, the four of us in that car. No motor, nobody had a motor and we off load before daylight there at Mr. Hilbert's. Push one of those skiffs in the water and pay him when you'd come back - just get in it and go! Well, two of us would go one way and two the other. We would be casting there when daylight came - even before daylight. Most of the time I'd fish with Mr. Fugler.

We'd fish down the lake casting to the shore line paddling as we went. And around 11:00, we'd be a couple of miles from where we'd gotten the boat. Mr. Fugler would say, "Bud", everybody called me "Bud" at that time, "...you know I believe those fish would do better on the other side". I'd say, "Yes sir, Mr. Bill".

False River was about a mile wide, but that didn't make any difference. I was 16 years old playing on the football team and I was pretty stout, I guess. I'd grab those oars up and across we'd have business. Once we'd get on the other side, we'd start fishing back toward the direction we'd come from. About 2:00, we'd be across from Mr. Hilbert's, might have a good bit of bass, sometimes not too many, but as Mr. Fugler was a good fisherman, I would watch him fish and I'd catch some too. Maybe about 2:00, Mr. Bill would say, "... well I guess it is time to go home". I would grab the oars and oar back across the river. I know one time in particular he and I had crossed the river, we had 19 real fine bass - the fellows on the other side only had two. They didn't feel like they wanted to make that pull. But that was nothing to me, I was glad to go and glad to get to paddle and everything else long as I could fish a little bit. So that was Mr. Bill Fugler.

Mr. Fugler made a lure. If you look at it now, you'd say that it is something like a lunker lure, but it was a double spinner outfit. If you pulled it fast, it would come across the top of the water, and at that time you had a lot of grass beds in False River and boy, you'd get some tremendous strikes and catch some good fish on it, too. That was Mr. Bill Fugler.

A limit catch by the author of False River bass.

FISHING TRIP TO BUZZARD BAYOU

I want to tell about a fishing trip that my father-in-law, George and I took one summer in the 50's. One of my coworkers at the refinery was bragging about all the bass he was catching, but he would not divulge his spot. I reminded him of a spot I had told him about once and he finally told me. He said the place had no name but he called it "Buzzard Bayou" He then described to me how to get there. He said to go west on Highway 190 to the Atchafalaya River, but not to cross the river, just head south. And he says, "you'll never find it, it's way down, - it's about 20 miles down the levee" Well, I told him, "I'll take that chance".

Well, we took off from George's house at the farm about 2 o'clock in the morning and we turned south on the gravel road that follows the levee and continued on pass Bayou Big Alabama and Bayou Little Alabama until we finally got to the end of the road - still no bayou, he said the bayou came to the levee.

As we were in a truck with the bateau in the bed of the truck, we continued riding on the bature of the levee. I don't think that my friend wanted me to find this spot, but he more or less felt obligated to tell me, but we were going to go as far as we could. Several miles pass the end of the gravel road, we came to a small opening at the edge of the levee. It looked like a watering hole for cattle really, it was about 12 feet wide and heavy with underbrush. I told George that this must be the spot, even though you could only see about 50 yards up this little slough . It was heavily covered with underbrush. He said, "well let's try it as we are here now and it's too late to turn back and try another place". We unloaded the bateau and our small two-horse motor and proceeded up this little slough. As we progressed, it never got any wider than about 30 feet and the branches of the trees nearly met in the middle. Practically all of our casts had to be side armed because of the overhanging brush.

Well, we proceeded to fish and started catching a few bass. At about 11 o'clock, we went back to the truck to fry a couple of bass and potatoes. George always carried his camp box with stove, pot, and skillet to cook a bite at noon. We never took a chance on not catching, he always had a couple of potatoes, a few eggs, a couple of cans of root beer and a loaf of bread. But this particular day we did have a few bass, so we fileted a couple of bass and peeled two potatoes and had a good meal along with a cup of coffee. As usual, after a little lunch, George always wanted to take a nap. He said, "Give me about an hour and come back and get me", as I was going back to fishing.

It was almost 1 o'clock when I started fishing again, terribly hot, but pretty soon, the fish began to strike. The sky clouded up and the wind was blowing - I knew a thunderstorm was approaching. The fish went on a feeding frenzy that I've never seen before. Those fish really went wild. I had never seen fish so aggressive in all my fishing career. All species bass, sac-a-lait, goggle eyed perch and catfish were hitting that Houser Hell Diver with a red and white skirt. Even though I had a gallon Thermos of ice water to drink in the boat, I was about to smother, but I could not stop casting. I was catching a fish virtually every cast. When I didn't get a strike, I was disappointed. I could hear that thunderstorm coming through the trees. My ice chest was full and I was throwing fish in the bottom of the boat.

Well, here comes the down pour, so I cranked up and got to the truck in a couple of minutes and ran and jumped in the cab. George said, with a laugh, "Why did you quit?" I said, "I didn't have anymore room to put anymore fish". And he said, "You must be joking".

So, when the rain slacked off, he went to look and he was amazed at the amount of fish and the variety. I had limits of both bass and sac-a-lait plus a number of goggle eye perch and a few catfish. I had 79 head of fish all total!

He said, "Let's get out of here as that levee is going to get slick", and it really did. We barely made it to the gravel section. Later, the summer rain set in and we weren't able to go back; then, the following year, there was some levee work done which messed up so called "Buzzard Bayou", but that was quite an experience.

Bass caught at "Buzzard Bayou"

OTHER WAYS TO CATCH BASS

Before I get into ways that I'm going to talk about, I want to talk about this particular place that some of these events took place. This was up the Red River at a place called Grassy Lake and I've mentioned Grassy Lake before because in the early days of the 50's, it was a wild and woolly place. The way to get to Grassy Lake was to launch your boat at a place called Three River and it was a 12-mile journey up the Red River. When you got to Grassy Lake, it was a pullover type place where you had to bring a small boat and you had to pull it over , I'd say at least 300 yards. It was one trip to haul the small boat over and then back to the river bank. Another trip to haul the small outboard and a little two gallon gas can and back again, and then to bring your fishing tackle.

After awhile, a lot of people, including me and my partner, would leave a small boat in the back, then all you would have to carry was your fishing tackle. We would turn the boat upside down and lock it to a tree and even lock a small motor to a tree and cover it with a piece of tarp. Now the down side of that, several people had boats stolen and we had one stolen. We had locked it to a tree, running a chain around the tree and then around the transom brace in the little boat. Well, we got there one day and the chain was still locked around the tree, but the boat was gone, they had broken the transom brace and we never did see that boat again.

When it really got popular, it was very common to see 25 or 30 boats stashed in the woods by people who did not want to portage over that long distance.

We saw several ways that people devised to keep others from stealing their boat. One fellow had a real ingenious way to do it. He had a little cypress skiff made out of relatively light cypress wood maybe a half inch. Along the sides, just below the water line at various places, he had drilled six holes, three on each side and what he did was bring with him six thermos bottle stoppers. You know the kind, if you press the little lever they expanded. When he would get ready to fish , he would pull his boat up on the shore, put his six stoppers in and go ahead and go fishing. When he got through fishing, he'd take his six thermal bottle stoppers out of the boat, let the boat sink, put them in his tackle box , go on back to the landing. And that was pretty ingenious I thought. But anyway, that's Grassy Lake.

So, I'm going to get into some ways that we caught fish that was a little out of the ordinary. I need to say, most of the veteran bass fishermen already know about catching bass by using a spoon or plastic frog and sliding it over grass beds or lilies. But I want to touch on a way that I've caught fish fishing in algae or what we call duck weed.

My old partner and I was fishing in a section of Grassy Lake called "Jeff Slough". "Jeff Slough" was a long finger of water that ran north and south and there was always some algae in that section. But on that particular trip, the west wind had been blowing hard for several days and all the algae was piled real heavy on the east side and it had about half the slough covered. We were fishing the west bank and so were several other boats, as this slough was about half a mile long but weren't having any luck. Several times I would hear a fish strike and look but would see no ripples. And after hearing several strikes, I looked across in time to see that mat of algae moved. I told my old fishing partner, Mr. Mack, I said, "Tie on the biggest top water plug you have" and he asked why. I said, "Mack, we are going to have some fun". We both tied on big Lucky 13 lures and I paddled within casting distance of the algae and we started casting. We would cast our plugs on that mat of thick algae and give it a few jerks to make it dig down to the water and what an explosion when those bass would hit that lure. Once hooked, the bass were free to fight as the line cut through the algae with no problem what so ever. On that particular trip, we caught 22 real large bass, with the biggest going over six pounds. That was one of the few times that we ever found algae so thick. It didn't matter what color the plug was as they were hitting at the movement on top of the algae. Mr. Mack said, "Boy, they hit that plug like a torpedo hits a battleship". I really like to fish patches of algae, but most of the time it is rather thin and that's when I used the plastic frog or spoon. Most of the time if fish are feeding near the surface, you will have pretty good luck.

I want to also touch on fishing over matted grass beds. I really prefer a spoon over the mouse type lures, you know the ones that float on the surface and they are more or less weedless. But I prefer the spoon because of the weight. A lot of times the bass, trying to hit through grass, will blow the lighter lure away, but the spoon, being heavier, the bass has a better chance to get it. Incidentally, I use a pork strip or grub on the hook and preferably white. If a grass bed is slightly under water, but not enough to use a top of the plug, I like to use a fast running lure like "Herb's Dilly" you know it's spoon-shaped with a little propeller on the front and when you pull it fast, it skirts across the top of the water and makes quite a commotion, When you use this lure, you need to keep it on top by reeling fast. And don't worry, he'll catch it if he wants it- I also use a trailer hook when fishing this lure, now, the down side is, generally when you hook a fish he will bury himself in the grass and you'll have to go to him.

Up there on that Red River, we use to fish a place that was across the river from the Grassy Lake, it was Sunk Lake. And in Sunk Lake you had large areas of lily pads in it and one way that we would fish it would be to cast a Herb's Dilly on the thickest part and start reeling the lure in. You could see the bass as they swam through the lily pad long roots or stems and as that lure hit an opening between the pad he would nail them. A lot of times they would tangle on the long stem or root and you would have to go in and get it. That, too, is exciting fishing.

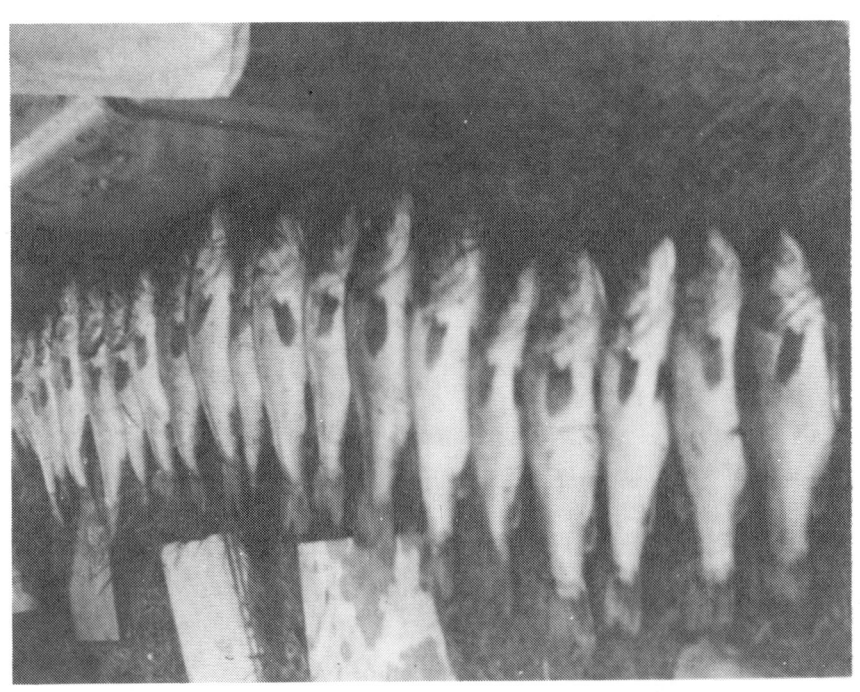

"Grassy Lake" bass caught by the author and "Mr. Mack"

My father-in-law, George, with our catch of huge "Sunk Lake" bass

NIGHT FISHING FOR BASS

Years ago, I used to fish at night quite a lot, especially during the hot summer months, June, July and August, when the temperature and humidity here in Louisiana was way up. Temperature in the 90's, humidity in the 60's or so. It was really a pleasure to go out after sundown. It would be quiet, most of the traffic would be gone, and a lot of times you have the lake, canal or whatever you were fishing all to yourself.

It doesn't really matter much whether the moon is shining or not. The moonlight only benefits the angler, of course, it is better because you can see the shoreline and see the objects you want to cast to. The nights I preferred were when there was a full moon or near a full moon with a cloudy, over cast sky.

This gave the water a kind of fluorescent look, it was better than if you had the full moon and no clouds. I always like to fish when it was over cast.

Speaking about what effect the moon has on the fish, I don't think it has any. I have fished on occasions in narrow impoundments, such as pits and canals, with no moon. It would be so black, so dark, you couldn't see your partner in the back of the boat and still we caught fish. You would cast out and listen for your lure to hit and then start to reel. Every once in a while take your flashlight, which if you were fishing with a partner, which I did sometimes, a lot of times by myself, shine and pick up the shore line, shine your flashlight beam over there, orient yourself again where to throw and go ahead and fish. A lot of times we did good even with no moon, but most of the time we tried to go when there was a moon.

I need to add, because I did some night fishing before the advent of the Hell Diver, it was the Shannon Twin Spinner which I've mentioned several times and I used to like to use the black and white buck tail or the solid white buck tail. Then, I had an occasion to fish with a friend one time, his favorite color was the yellow buck tail. He said it just gave off a pretty glow in the water at night.

False River is where I did a lot of night fishing at Mr. Hilbert's camp. In those days, they didn't have any boat ramps. Very few people had a trailer, I don't remember anybody having a trailer. Some people would have car top racks and bring a small boat. But most of the time, I believe I have covered some of this before, you'd go to one or two places that had several wooden skiffs and you just pulled up there any time you felt like it, it could be in the middle of the night and take your little motor down the hill and put it on the boat and go fishing. You'd pay the man the next morning. It was 50 cents to use a boat.

During those times, I was working at a local refinery and had to do some shift work. So many a nights I would get off at 11:00 and if I was anticipating going I would have my little motor and tackle in the trunk of my car and I'd take off and go fishing. But other times if I didn't anticipate going, I'd go home and maybe on the way home see how pretty the moon was and the weather was I'd just go there and load up and it wasn't a long ways to go about 45 miles. I would fish until daylight. At daylight I'd fish for an hour or so and probably catch some fish then also. And my favorite lure which I spoke about describing some of the old lures was the Howser Hell Diver with the black and white skirt. Sometimes, when they'd be biting real good, I'd tie on the top water lure and try to catch one on top just for the thrill of it. But most of the time I'd fall back on that spinner bait because it would out catch a top water lure 10 to 1. It was a real good lure for night fishing.

In regards to night fishing, what I need to say is, if you haven't tried it, you need to do so because it will be nice and cool and quiet. Most of the time you will not have a lot of boat traffic. Once you get into it and see how really pleasurable it is, I'll think you will enjoy it.

False River bass caught at night by the author.

HOOKED FISHERMAN (ABOUT LAKE SUTTON)

In the early 1940's, my dad & I went to a place called Lake Sutton. It is located northwest of Simmesport, LA, in an area called the "big bend" area. This place is about 75 miles northwest of Baton Rouge, LA, and was a long way to travel in a 1934 Ford. We had gone to Lake Sutton before - 4 fisherman in one car - due to gas rationing, etc. - and on this trip my dad had caught a 5 pound bass, which was a large one in those days.

We had to drive through a farmer's yard to get to the lake, and the last time we were there, the car got stuck trying to get from the gravel road to the lake, which was about a 300 yard route through the field and the woods. So in planning this trip, we watched the weather to be sure the trail would be dry.

We stopped at the farmer's house just about daylight and paid him for the use of one of his skiffs - I think he had three skiffs. We loaded our fishing tackle into the skiff and had to paddle a trail through the marsh grass to get to the lake, that was about a 100 yards from shore. It was a shallow lake with several duck blinds in it.

We started casting and we noticed one other boat on the lake. After an hour or so, our boats came into the same general area of the lake. We could see it was a man and his little son fishing from that boat and they were both casting.

After a while, I glanced over at their boat and could see the man pulling at something on his back. I told my dad, "I believe that little boy hooked his dad". We paddled over and inquired if he needed help. He said he believed that the plug was just caught in his shirt. We put our boat next to his and my Dad saw that the hook was in the flesh of the man's back just under his shoulder blade! My dad cut his shirt and tried to pull the hook out , but the man cried out in pain and the little boy subsequently fainted and fell in the bottom of the boat!

We immediately switched our attention from the hooked man to the fainted little boy. We had a gallon "thermos" of cold water which we used to revive the little boy, who "came to" crying. As we positioned the boat to attend to the boy, that put me near the man with the hook in his back. I cut the line and unscrewed the treble hook from the lure. The hook was buried up to the bend. I had a pair of side cutter pliers in my tackle box and I got a hold of the hook, and with a twisting motion, made the point of the hook and the barb make an 180° turn and break through the skin, then it was a simple matter to cut the point and barb off and back the hook out of the skin.

The only damage to the man's back was two small holes where the hook had gone in and come out. I put 2 drops of iodine on these spots and told him to get a tetanus shot when he got to town. We gave them ice water and afterwards, the man tied a single hook to the little boy's line.

We did a good deed that day as it would have been a long, uncomfortable journey to have that hook removed.

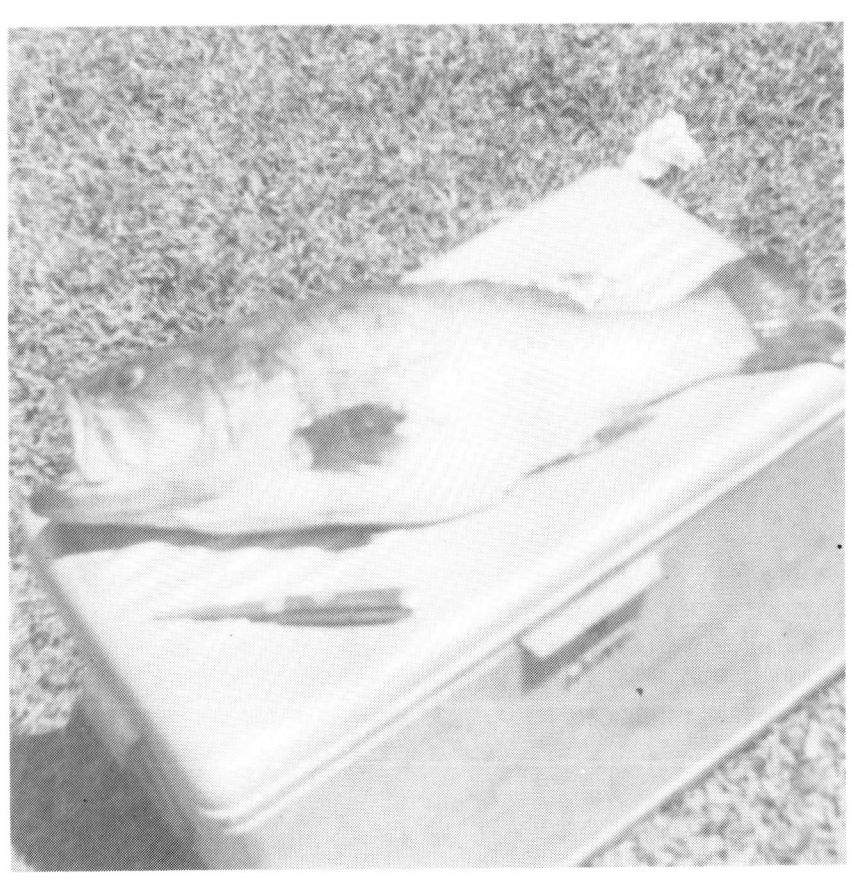

This huge bass caught by the author on a "Herb's Dilly" on top at the Morganza Pits

CATCHING WHITE BASS

Anyone who has ever caught white bass knows how much fun that can be especially if the fish are schooling. I want to tell of a few places and ways that I have caught them. One place that I used to fish is at "Old River" locks above Simmesport. We would launch a small boat and go into the section of "Old River" that is more like a lake now because of the locks. We fished for bass early in the morning but kept an eye out and watched for when the white bass would start to strike on the surface. When we would see the commotion, we would immediately crank up and head for the school. They would be feeding on the surface on small shad and then submerge to come up at another location. We would always keep an eye out for where they were going to come up again and rush to that spot.

We always had two rods, one with a top water lure tied on and another with a underwater lure. For the top water lure, I prefer a tiny torpedo, either silver and black or shad colored. For the underwater lure, I would use a "Little George" which is kind of a lead head jig with a spinner on the tail or a small hot spot or small spoon. The little hot spot plug I would prefer either the black shad color or the shad color with a blue back. I liked to use a top water lure when they were feeding on the top. When they go down, you'd use a underwater lure. And it's common to catch two on a lure at the same time. I've seen 10 or 15 fish following the one that was hooked, trying to get the lure away from it..

One method we used was to keep the fish in the water until your partner could get his lure in the water. I've had occasions to have a fish on at the boat and pick up my other rod and thrush it in the water and I'd have a fish on both rods.

Another place I've had luck in catching white bass is in the Atchafalaya River on the points where the rivers and the canals branch off. They are always in the current on the downstream side. Grand Lake is also a good place to catch white bass where Bayou Pigeon enters the Lake. At one time, I had placed sixth in the record book for White Bass, I have that fish mounted on my den wall. It weighed 2 lbs. 11 oz. And at that time, that was a pretty good size white bass.

The author with a white bass, weighing 2 lbs., 11 ozs.

OUTDOOR ARTICLES

THE ATCHAFALAYA BASIN

The Atchafalaya Basin is approximately 600,000 acres. It has more than 40 public boat launches and quite a few private launches, also. There are literally thousands of bayous and canals. It extends from Pointe Coupee Parish above highway 190 to near Morgan City in St. Mary Parish, to the south of highway 90. It runs north/northwest to south/southeast and is approximately 80 miles long and 15 miles wide, The basin is contained by levees on both sides There are several bayous that lead off the river to the east and west guide levees. I-10 Causeway cuts across the basin near the north end on its route from Baton Rouge to Lafayette. On the west side of the basin, some of the larger lakes are Lake Henderson and it's chain of smaller lakes and there is Lost Lake, Cow Island Lake and many other lakes.

Whiskey Bay Pilot Channel and the Atchafalaya River split above Butte LaRose and come back together at Lake Mongoulis. Near the intersection, there is access to the east levy through Upper Grand River and access to the west guide levy through Bayou Crook Chene. The next access to the east guide levee is at the Bayou Sorrel cut, that is where my camp is located.

Off of Bayou Sorrel, there are numerous hunting and fishing lakes, bayous and canals. South of the Bayou Sorrel junction on the west side is an arm of Grand Lake and Buffalo Cove and other lakes and canals; and many, many bayous and canals The river then flows generally south into Grand Lake, Six Mile Lake, Flat Lake and by Morgan City to Atchafalaya Bay and finally to the Gulf. South of Bayou Sorrel on the east side of the Atchafalaya River is Lake Murphy, Big Bayou Pigeon, Little Bayou Pigeon and a huge area of Grand Lake that was "diked" off years ago to keep sediment from building up in the Basin. There are literally hundreds of canals and bayous.

Next, going south, there is Old River, Bayou Long, Willow Cove, Duck Lake and many, many more. All this, also, ends up at Six Mile Lake and Flat Lake. It is very, very easy to get lost in this maze of canals and bayous. Even with a map, you will get lost because a lot of the canals and bayous that you see on the map are either silted up or clogged with vegetation. It is advisable to go in this area with someone who knows it. I have hunted and fished in a good part of these areas in years gone by, but I mostly hunt and fish near my camp now.

At one time there was a causeway proposed to cross the Basin from Bayou Sorrel south/southwest to Charenton on the west side. It would have been approximately 20 miles long The project was started with the clearing of timber and brush, but was canceled when the individual who was undertaking this project ran out of money. This incident was related to me by several old timers of the area. It is interesting to draw a line on the map of the Basin and visualize this project.

The old-timers tell me that from above the Sorrel cut south it was a lake several miles wide and six or eight miles long instead of the channel it is today. There were six or eight light houses to guide boats across Grand Lake. All that is accretion land now made up by silt carried down the river. This Basin is something to see. I need to add that in the Basin there are several wild life management areas, and they are open to the public.

There are a few guidelines for the use of these areas such as where to camp, where to park and the time of the day that you can primarily hunt in these areas. Now, most of the land in the Basin ,I would say, is privately owned. The State has a considerable amount of land also and at this time is trying to purchase and acquire more so that in the years to come there will be some tremendous acreage of land for public use.

"THE OLD SWAMPER"

I'm at the camp tonight, I want to write something about Alcide Verrett, "the old swamper", affectionately known as Uncle Alcide. I'm going to start because right now I'm next to his old house which is now really in a shamble.

The way I met Uncle Alcide was pretty ordinary as I had passed his place a many, many a morning, but I didn't know him and I hadn't stopped. That was when I was hunting below his place down the Atchafalaya to a place called the Arm of Grand Lake. I also fished down there near the Amarada Pumping Station.

As time went by, I finally had the use of a facility below Uncle Alcide's place, it was just a shack, but we were able to have the permission of a man who formerly owned it to use it. Believe me, it was just a shack. But we made do with it, made a couple of hunting seasons out of it and it was really the bare necessity.

One day, I was getting ready to cross the canal from this little shack and Uncle Alcidecame drifting by in his bateau. He stopped, and I said, "You must be Mr. Verrett". He said, "Yes I am.". I said, "I'm Bud Oliver." He said, "Well, I've seen your boat a number of times, of course, I hadn't met you." We talked for a few minutes and then he was on his way to tend his nets. I was going to try to catch a bass. He told me, "The next time you're up my way, stop by the camp and we'll have some coffee". I told him I would.

Sure enough, the next time I was out, I stopped by and visited with Uncle Alcide and we developed a friendship. By and by, I stopped and chatted with him a number of times then I asked what would be the possibility of putting a camp on the hill next to him. He said, "well what you need to do is get permission from the land owner and see what they will say about it". I need to say right now that the reason that I was asking about permission to put a camp next to him was because the little facility we were using had been destroyed by vandals. Got there one day and someone had broke open the door, which was not very substantial, and overturned what little furniture we had and threw my mattress out in the back water, broke up the bed and turned over the little cast iron stove, broke a mirror and did a lot of damage.

So when this happened, I went down to Uncle Alcide and told him what had happened. He said "Well Bud, whatever you can salvage, bring it down here and put it in my barn". (He called his little shed a barn). "Then later on maybe you can find a place and I'll keep it here for you until that time comes". So sure enough, we did it.

Then came the conversation of trying to get permission from the landowner to build next to him. So, as luck would have it one day I was out on his porch talking with him and a representative of the people who owned the land stopped by. They do that regularly to check on the land. I was there and I asked this individual, "What's the chances of getting a campsite lease?" He said, "I believe we can work something out", he says "I'll look into it for you" "Well," I said "in the meantime would it be okay to put a tent up?". He says, "yes, but don't build anything permanent until you hear from me".

Sure enough, my son-in-law, Chet, and I, we put up a tent and a lean to, and we had it up for about four or five months. We made a duck season out of it, it served the purpose, it was okay. We spent some pretty bad nights in there with the weather. In fact, one night I was in the tent by myself and a storm came up. I was pretty concerned because there was a lot of pieces of loose tin laying around and I was thinking, well, maybe one of those pieces of tin will come through this tent and I would get seriously hurt.

Well it was about 1 o'clock in the morning and the storm kind of let up and I looked over and Uncle Alcide's light was on. I got up and put my clothes on. The rain stopped for a short time. I went and checked my boat to be sure that the bilge pump was working and it was. I went next door to Uncle Alcide and I said, "You know, this is pretty bad, I believe I'll come and finish the night with you". He said, "Well great, come on." He said, "that back bedroom is empty." So I took my sleeping bag and I went next door and got in the back bedroom of Uncle Alcide's trailer.

Of course, the wind came up again and I didn't know if I had made the right choice or not because the back end of that trailer was shaking quite a lot. Anyway, we made the night and everything was all right .

During the duck season, "Chet" and I would set our alarm for 4:00 a.m., crawl out of our sleeping bags and fire up the lanterns and stove to make coffee. It was pretty damp and cold under our lean to as we got ready to go to the swamp, when out of the darkness, we would hear Uncle Alcide's voice call out, "Coffee and biscuits are ready boys". "Chet" would exclaim, with a big smile, "It don't get any better than this". Those big "cathead" biscuits with real butter sure did taste good with a big cup of coffee. Not too good for your cholesterol, but they were fine to the taste buds!.

So, I did get permission after about six months. The gentleman called me and said if you want to have a camp lease meet me in Baton Rouge and he gave me the name of the motel. I met him and signed a little lease, and it was just a nominal fee but you had to keep the place up and it was for a year at a time. So that started the deal where I was going to finally build a camp.

I need to add that where I had my little tent set up was like a jungle. We began to clear it out a little bit. Every time I'd come back, Uncle Alcide had cut down quite a few trees, and cleared quite a bit of brush to help me to get my camp ready. Sure enough, when we got the land more or less cleared, I ordered some material and I pre-fabed my camp at my house in Baton Rouge, hauled it out a piece at a time and I kept a log and it took me 40 trips from Baton Rouge to get the camp erected, it took about four months I believe. About a year later, I put a screen porch on it. It worked out pretty good.

I need to add Uncle Alcide always had a camp full of company and he cooked a big meal <u>every</u> day. He would always insist that you ate. He had the main course and he had desserts.

Here this gentleman was in the middle of the Atchafalaya swamp, cooking these fantastic meals for his friends.

There has been times on a Sunday when there would be a dozen boats tied up to his place with people, some of the old-timers and their wives would come to have Sunday dinner. And Uncle Alcide, that was really the prime of his life, was to have people over and cook a big meal for them.

Well I tell you, he was one of the finest people I've ever met and I spent a many a many night in the years that I've had this camp. he would be over here at my place or I would be over at his place and we would talk till 10 or 11 o'clock at night. He told me a wealth of stories about the Atchafalaya Basin and the way that he worked and made his living here. He spent virtually his whole life in this swamp. He said though, even through the depression, he never lacked for anything since he hunted and fished. He fished commercially, he trapped commercially, and he also logged. Over the years, he divulged all these stories to me. I might be a little redundant on some of these things because I've talked about him previously in this book, about finding beehives and raiding the beehives for the honey and the wax. The wax, he told me, would be sold to the Government, they used bee's wax in some of their military shells I understand. So even though when the depression was on, that didn't matter. He and his family never lacked of food, he raised a big garden, he had fruit trees and even when crawfish was selling for four cents a pound he said he made money. He caught his bait, he ran his traps with his pirogue. It took very little gasoline to bring his catch in.

Also with his trapping, he would run his trap lines and skin his fur out, roll it up and freeze it in his freezer. He had a gas butane freezer and then when he had enough furs to make a trip in, he would bring them in to the dealer. There was never a lack of food. He said there were some wild hogs around. They'd kill a hog, render it out, make sausage and meatballs, put it down in a crock and cover the meat with the hog lard and it would keep indefinitely.

During the hunting season, he would bag ducks and geese, squirrels and rabbits, and deer, and that was the meat he needed. What was not used immediately was smoked in his smoke house. The only thing he really needed money for was for staples. He would buy sugar, coffee and flour. He would buy it in large quantities.

He also told me about the loss of his family out here in the Basin. He was out fishing, making a living and his wife and two children were living at his camp. Some how or another, his wife sent out to the store because there was a community out here in this Basin at that time with a schoolhouse and a store, they did quite a lot of farming- She sent or she went to get some kerosene. for the stove. By mistake, she was sold gasoline instead, and when she got back to the camp and tried to pour the gas in the container for the stove, it ignited and it burned up the whole family. Sad to say, the wife and the two children lost their lives And when Uncle Alcide came in from fishing that day, he had lost <u>everything</u>. He told me the only thing he had left was the wet pair of coveralls that he was wearing. Everything else was gone.

But he lived through that. He talked about it and he didn't mind talking about it. He rallied from that disaster and went on with his life.

Some time later, he remarried. He remarried a nice lady and he built a five room house on the banks of the Atchafalaya, very near where he had spent his lifetime. He stayed there and fished commercially and trapped. Occasionally he'd take a little job down at one of the Pumping Stations just to do a little work when maybe the fishing was off a little bit. And he would tell me tales about the river. I'm telling you, in hindsight, what I would have given now to have recorded those 10 or 12 years I had talking with and listening to this man of the knowledge he had of this great Basin.

He told one time about being lost an the river when he almost froze to death. He was working down below his house at the Amarada Pumping Station. He was on the 3 to 11 shift. When time came for him to get off, the fog had set in and it was a freezing rain, but he told his workers he could make it and if he didn't come, his wife would be worried about him So he attempted to get home. Well, some way or another he got turned around on the river and instead of getting to his place in 30 minutes or so, he was four or five hours getting back because he had gotten turned around in the fog and gone way, way out of the way until he saw a landmark and was able to get himself straightened out, But he did and when he got to his house on the river, his clothes were frozen to him and his wife had to come to him and help him out of the boat. She was waiting up even though it was in the early hours in the morning and had a good fire going. He survived that ordeal pretty good.

You would have to have known Uncle Alcide to appreciate everything that he did for people. When he and his wife set up housekeeping here, she told him, "Alcide, we have to build a boat to take people in who get sick out here." There were a lot of families out here at the time which there are not any now. He said, "that's a good idea" So he built a boat that could be used for taking sick people to the landing. It was a huge cypress hull boat with a cab on it and he installed a Jeep motor in it. He had bunks that would fold down. They did, on several occasions, take children and anybody else who needed transportation to the levee because it was pretty primitive out there at that time.

I need to say about Uncle Alcide, when I would come out, I would always bring him a newspaper. He would take that paper and read the fine print without eyeglasses. Now, here was a man, at that time, in his mid-80's, and he could shoot his rifle and read a newspaper without glasses.

As long as his company came, he was happy. I need to say, as years went by, and the last few years he was out here, the company started to dwindle. Some of his old friends "passed away" and he didn't have the company he used to have. I got here one time and he was pretty down-hearted, and I said, "Uncle Alcide, what's the matter?" In fact, it was a Monday. He said,

"You know, I had all that food cooked yesterday (Sunday) and nobody showed up". It really, really hurt him and I felt truly sorry about that.

But he would tell me tales about fishing, hunting and cutting timber, on and on. The way he set his traps, the way he set his set lines. It was just amazing, the stories he would tell. I got to listen to these for more than 10 years. That was every week. If I would have had the foresight to record these, they would be something worthwhile. In his later years, after he got well into his 80's, about 85 or so, he started having a little problem. He started hallucinating a little, and he eventually had to go live in town. That was a sad day for me because I used to feel bad when I came out and he wasn't there, and that was just for one trip. So now, for the last four years, well, he is never here anymore. He had spent several years in town at his brother's house. But, year before last, he "passed away". His old place, like I mentioned at the beginning of this story, is in shambles now- it is completely rotted down.

I want to say about that fine gentleman, I never hope or expect to meet anybody any more of a gentleman than Uncle Alcide. I really, really enjoyed the friendship I had with him and it was a pleasure to have known him.

"The Old Swamper", Alcide Verret, at right, sitting with the author on the author's porch.

SWAMP NEIGHBORS

This is about the people who now hunt, fish and camp where my camp is located.

First there is Guy Allen. Guy owns a house boat across the canal from my camp. He is still employed, but will retire next year. He hunts with his young son, Matthew, and with his grandson, Luke. He also fishes recreationally with nets and cross lines. He is a good hunter and fisherman and really knows his way around the swamp.

Then, there is Percy "Junior" Wisdom. "Junior" has a camp on the bank of the canal across from my camp. "Junior" has the reputation of being the best squirrel hunter in those parts; and he proves it every season. He also is a good rabbit hunter. "Junior" is retired, but he still fishes commercially.

Next, there is Maxwell "Bun" Allen. "Bun" is his nickname. He is Guy Allen's brother and he also has a camp on the bank of the canal. His camp is located up the hill from Guy's houseboat. "Bun" is mostly a deer and squirrel hunter and gets his limit most every season. His hunting buddies are "Ron" Lawson and "Bun's" nephew, Scott Allen. These three are real good hunters and they give me deer meat all the time.

Incidentally, my camp is the only camp on the south side of the canal since my old friend Alcide "passed away". I am the elder of the group by about 15 years. They are always offering to give me a hand if I need assistance. I'm not a native of that area as I was born and raised in Baton Rouge. All these folks, as well as their parents, have always been connected to the swamp. These folks, even though they will help anyone who needs help, take awhile before they really accept you as "one of them". They brag on my duck hunting ability whether I deserve it or not, but I usually get my limit. So far, at 75, 1 can still do everything in the swamp for myself, but it is a good feeling to know that I can call on any one of these guys and they will not hesitate to give me a hand.

"Red" Cowart is also a camp neighbor, although, like me, he is an outsider. He has had a camp in that area for more than 30 years. "Red" worked for Jacob's Constructors & Engineers when I was construction manager. He is another person that will help anyone if they need help. He is always accompanied by his man "Friday", Raymond Hill.

Another one of my neighbors is Huey Martinez. He is a local crawfish dealer and has a houseboat that he brings out for the hunting season.

Swamp neighbors, from left, Guy Allen, Scott Allen, Percy "Jr." Wisdom, and Maxwell "Bun" Allen, having a hot meal at the author's camp.

"Bun" Allen and Ron Lawson in front of "Bun's" camp.
Two top notch deer and squirrel hunters!

Two real "swampers", Raymond Hill and "Red" Cowart, in front of "Red's" camp on the bank of the Atchafalaya River.

The best squirrel hunter in this area, "Jr." Wisdom, on his camp porch.

The author's boat tied up to Guy Allen's camp boat.

TEXAS "GREEN HORNS" TO THE SWAMP

I recently had occasion, after many attempts, to take my sister, Joyce, and her daughter, Scarlett (named so because of her beautiful red hair) to my camp in the Atchafalaya Basin. They were in Baton Rouge from Dallas as we had some family business to handle. We planned to leave quite early as the afternoon temperature gets in the 90's this time of year. So, we planned to depart at 7:30 a.m , and I was asked to give them a "wake up call" when I got up and I did so.

I had "drafted" my daughter, Patricia, born on St. Patrick's day, to come along as she is a good deck hand, so she arranged her busy schedule to come with us.

I had procured cold drinks, sandwich materials, chips and dips and the usual, along with ice and water, and we took off in my car pulling my boat. Incidentally, I "bent the rules", as I never take more than two passengers in my boat as it is a high performance hull and it doesn't perform very well with a load.

We arrived at the boat launch at Bayou Sorrel after passing through Plaquemine, LA, where I showed them one of the construction sites that I helped build as "resident construction manager", a massive undertaking.

We launched the boat and everyone, life preservers on, boarded, then it was about a 15 minute boat ride to my camp on the canal at the Atchafalaya River. The ride was pleasant and at about ¾ throttle, we were making 45 mph. It was a beautiful morning and we unloaded everything at the camp then I picked up my key to the gate in the slough that leads to "Sawyer's Cove". "Sawyer's Cove" is privately leased, but I am a friend of that gentleman and he issued me a key.

It is quite a chore to go through that gate, as the slough is only about 25' wide and the gate is quite heavy and about 19' of boat, including the motor, is quite difficult to maneuver, but we were lucky as there was no current and with some twisting and turning, we were able to open the gate, go through it and re-lock it. Re-locking the gate is required by the lessee.

Going through the slough, we were able to observe a large owl up close. It was not afraid of us.

We arrived at "Sawyer's Cove", a beautiful body of water surrounded by cypress trees, that makes one think of pre-historic times. I need to add here that I take credit, whether I deserve it or not, for the "Cove" being what it is today and still in existence. At one time, the Corps of Engineers proposed cutting a canal diagonally across the "cove" to expedite the flow of water. When I found out about this plan, I sent letters to quite a few senators and representatives, both state and federal, requesting that this operation be canceled as it would destroy this pristine spot. After much correspondence and especially with one influential senator, I received a letter from one of the "powers that be" with the Corps that informed me the project would be canceled. I was very happy about that decision.

Now, back to the outing. As we entered the "cove", we met a crawfisherman that I know. He was raising has traps and he told me to raise a few traps to show my guests how the crawfish were harvested, which I did. The guests were elated and took several pictures of the traps and the fisherman. I explained to them that where we were motoring, in about 6 feet of water, would be completely dry this fall, with weeds growing here.

We continued further into the "cove", which is about one mile long, to the head of the "cove" where I showed them one of the duck blinds we use, which was barely above the water line. We observed osprey and water turkeys in their natural habitat. On our way out of the cove, we saw "Pete" with several other crawfisherman and we stopped to chat with them. They informed us they had 17 sacks of crawfish - a pretty decent catch, but certainly not exceptional.

Then it was back through the gate, unlocking and locking, and headed back to my camp, but instead of stopping at the camp, we went out into the Atchafalaya River and went down river to the

Phillips canal, where I had them to walk over a "dump" so that I could show them one of my "pullover" fishing holes. They said it looked like a jungle. I told them that very few people know about this good fishing hole and that's the reason why I can catch such beautiful bass, fishing out of my pirogue - it is a tough pull.

Then we motored into a canal that leads to "Crossing Cove" which is slowly being taken over by willow trees. In fact, eventually all of the lakes will be taken over as silt is deposited every year and the lakes get smaller and smaller.

We went back to the camp and relaxed a bit. I dipped water out of the bayou for my tomato plants as we had not received rain in 28 days - a record!. I then asked my niece, Scarlett, if she wanted to take a boat ride with her "old uncle" and she said she would be delighted. Her mother cautioned her to "watch out -he used to race boats". We cranked up and made several passes in front of the camp and, of course, Patricia and Joyce watched us pass. I got that old Allison up near 60 MPH. If you trim the motor out properly, it will run fast, but it's kind of on the "wild side". I asked Scarlett if she wanted to drive it and she said she would. I had to explain about the trim switch and how it controlled the attitude of the hull. She soon got the feel of it and got the speed up to 46 mph but didn't want to go any faster. We had a good ride.

Later, I shared with my guests something quite interesting. Every year, in a tennis shoe that I have hanging on the outside wall of my camp, a warbler and her mate build a nest, lay 5 eggs and hatch some "chicks". I took the nest down very carefully and showed them the four little olive green birds nesting in the shoe. These warblers had just hatched out only a few days before. This is the fourth year they have occupied that shoe. At the end of the hatch, I usually clean it out for next year. My guests took pictures of the nest and its occupants also.

Then it was back to the camp and time for lunch, which consisted of sandwiches and snacks - all real tasty. After lunch, it was time for rifle and pistol practice behind the camp. The "girls" did really well with the .22, but not too good with the 9mm pistol - too much recoil.

It was beginning to get hot and as they had a long drive back to Dallas, we decided to leave so they could get ahead of the traffic. The boat ride back to the landing was pleasant, with the exception of meeting a tug pushing a heavily-loaded barge. It disturbed the water for several miles and we had to "take it slow", but then we were able to get back up to running speed and to the landing.

We loaded up and got back to town in good fashion. Patricia and I bid them "farewell" and they proceeded to Texas for their return trip home.

Although my sister and her daughter have traveled extensively world-wide, I don't believe they have seen anything like we showed them or been anywhere like they were taken on this "swamp trip". I know they enjoyed the day, and Patricia and I enjoyed taking them.

Beautiful Sawyer's Cove.

ANOTHER HUNT AT POINT AU FER

I had a three day weekend coming up and the weather was changing, so I decided to go down to Point au Fer and make a duck hunt with my friend and neighbor, Mr. "Cub".

I have written previously about this place and also "Cub", I had a standing invitation to come down any time he was at the camp.

I proceeded to get my gear together and at a early hour, "Rusty", my retriever and I left Baton Rouge. A lot of folks have found the logistics of this trip interesting so I'll discuss it in order in which it unfolds.

I leave Baton Rouge on I-10 interstate and cross the Mississippi River to Port Allen, LA, and then proceed south on LA 1, through Plaquemine, LA, to White Castle, LA, then turn on to Hwy. 69, to Hwy. 70 through Pierre Part, LA, where you cross over "Grand River" and continue south pass Lake Verret and Lake Palourde, on to Morgan City, LA. At Morgan City, you take Hwy. 90 to Amelia, LA, where the boat launch is located. This launch is pretty unique because you pull your boat trailer to the launching point where there is a steel lifting rig operated by an attendant, who places 2 huge nylon slings or straps under the boat. He then activates the electric motor which powers the lift and your boat is then lifted off the trailer and neatly placed on the water's surface.

Well, this leg of the trip, Baton Rouge to Amelia, is approximately 75 miles and takes about 2 hours travel time, which includes the launching of the boat. Then, its time to crank up and head off for a 45 mile boat ride to Mr. Cub's camp.

I leave the marina which is located on Bayou Boeuf and proceed in a southerly direction to Bayou Chene, which is part of the Intercoastal Waterway System and then pass Avoca Island. At this point, I need to say something about Avoca Island. It is not technically an island any longer due to the Great Flood of 1927 which inundated it. It was a huge farming area. The smoke stack of the sugar mill still stands as a testimonial to that era. It is privately owned and almost all of its 16,000 acres are covered by water.

My friend, "Cub" who was a friend of the caretaker of the island and the facilities was given a lifetime membership to fish there, so one morning we took off to make a fishing trip.

We crossed the ferry and arrived at the caretaker house. He told us he would show us where the boat launch was located. He said it was near the "boy scout camp". We followed him about a mile to the launch, and, at that point, never having been there, I asked Mr. George, (I don't recall his last name), where was the best place to fish. He said, "Anywhere you see 'good water'". I cranked up and idled down a small canal and we started fishing. We had caught a couple of fish and the canal ended at a large flat area of water with huge cypress tress scattered about.

I told "Cub", "This looks like a place I used to fish on the "Red River" - "Sunk Lake". Do you want to try it?" He said, "Go ahead". It was shallow, so I raised the outboard motor and proceeded with the trolling motor. Soon, we really hit a bonanza! We caught really big bass at all of the cypress trees. We limited out - so much that our 54 quart ice chest would hold only about half the fish caught. We left the boat at the "boy scout camp' and went home that day. The next day, we were back again and made another limit catch of those huge bass. Needless to say, we fished there for several more years, but I found a better way to get there - by boat from Bayou Chene. It remained a fantastic place to fish until the water hyacinths took over.

Back to the hunting trip, after passing Avoca Island, it was on past Lake Gascha. This is the point where you leave the Intercoastal Waterway and go into "Little Horn Bayou" and one of my land marks, a trapper's camp. Incidentally, at this point, you have traveled about 15 miles by water and then, for the next 30 miles, you will see virtually no boats.

I need to add that on that particular day, the route I have just described was a blaze of fall colors. The sun was extremely bright and the tupelo gum trees were aglow with the crimson, orange, purple, and yellow leaves of Fall. It was a sight to behold.

I mentioned a land mark - land marks were very important because of the maze of canals, bayous and bays that you have to negotiate. It is very easy to become lost.

Continuing on, then its a turn into a pipeline canal, and after passing many intersections, its into "Crooked Bayou" where Mr. "Cub's" friend had the house boat originally located. (Sometime later, the houseboat was moved as the lease for this location was terminated). I proceed down "Crooked Bayou" to "Atchafalaya Bay". This is a huge expanse of water. The bay is shallow, however, you can follow the shoreline as the landowners have excavated along the shore line and deposited the spoil on shore to help stop the land erosion and loss as the land is continuously being eroded.

You follow every turn in the shore line keeping about 150' off shore, and then its into "Creole Pass" which is a pass between the mainland and "Halter's Island", where a light house is located.

As I exited "Creole Pass", I would always stop and put my rain suit on because I knew I would be wet with spray when I crossed "Four League Bay".

Coming out of "Creole Pass", I would continue following the shore line for about 2 miles to "Shell Point", and then it was about 4 miles across "Four League Bay". I was lucky as I always found the water calm enough to cross, but I know of some boaters who had to turn back because of rough water. In order to cross the bay, as you could not see any landmarks, I would set a compass course of 205° S/SW, and about one half of the way across, you could just barely see the trapper's camp at the mouth of the small canal which you needed to enter.

So far on this trip, I had seen no boats, but half the way across "Four League Bay", I saw a large cruiser approaching. I recognized the boat as "Taddy" Aycock's 26' inboard, all aluminum cabin boat. We stopped and chatted for a few minutes and he told me, "Cub will really be glad to see you as when I left, he was alone". We said 'goodbye' and I proceeded on into the canal by the trapper's camp, where I then took off my rain suit.

After a couple of miles down this little bayou, I had to cross this little bay, approximately ¾ miles wide. As the surrounding terrain is very flat, it is extremely difficult to locate by sight the bayou on the other side of the bay, but I would usually "feel my way" to it. Maybe a tall bunch of roseau cane or marsh grass would guide me to the spot.

Now, down another bayou for a few miles to Lake Chapeau which is about 2 miles wide and then, into "Locust Bayou". You follow "Locust Bayou" to the Texaco Canal for a couple of miles, and finally, you are at the houseboat.

As I neared the house boat, I saw "Cub" come out on the walk, and when he recognized me, an "ear to ear" grin popped out on his face! I stayed 3 days that particular trip. We had some fantastic hunts in the mornings and good fishing in the afternoons.

Just before I left to come home and back to work, some other guests arrived.

After describing this trip, maybe you will also question my sanity for making this trip alone many times, however, when you love to hunt and fish, you sometimes take chances.

A SAD EXPERIENCE

In October, 1975, my neighbor and hunting friend, "Cub" Roberts, was planning to go to the marsh at Point Au Fer, LA, (that's south of Morgan City, LA) to work on duck blinds. He had an interest in a duck lease along with several other men.

Mr. "Cub" was retired and I was still working. He had torn down a fence and had a lot of good boards to use in making duck blinds. He told me, "Bud, I'm going to leave Friday morning to go to the camp and bring a load of lumber. Why don't you come Saturday morning?" I said that I would, so he left a load of lumber by the fence for me to bring on Saturday.

Well, Friday morning, I heard him crank up as his driveway was next to my bedroom window. It was about 4:00 a.m.. I went to work that day and later that afternoon, I loaded my truck with the lumber and hooked up my boat as to get an early start for Saturday morning. I set my clock for 4:00 a.m. as it was about a 75 mile trip by car and then a 45 mile boat ride from the launch at Amelia, LA.

I went to bed early and about 3:30 a.m. the phone rang. I thought it was the alarm clock, however, it was the St. Mary Parish Sheriff, Chester Baudoin, asking if I was Mr. Roberts' neighbor. I told him that I was. He then informed me that my friend, Mr. Roberts, had suffered a heart attack and died at the camp and for me not to come.

I waited until daylight and had the awful task of going next door and telling his wife the sad news.

I miss "Cub" as he was a good man. I think of him often. I was one of the pallbearers at his funeral.

If I hadn't been contacted by Sheriff Baudoin, I probably would have met his friends about ½ way, bringing his body out - What a sad experience.

DUCK HUNTING FEVER

People who do not love duck hunting cannot understand why we go through the hardships and expense to hunt ducks. After all the preparations are made, possibly weeks in advance, we set the alarm clock for 2:00 in the morning, get out of a warm bed, drive a couple of hours to the launch site to launch our boat. Then, probably a 30-minute boat ride in an open boat with the temperature near or below freezing to the marsh or swamp where we will hunt. Then it is a walk through the swamp or the woods with hip boots to where the pirogue is stashed. Another 30 minutes or ½ mile of paddling, all before daylight. And if the ducks are working that morning a good hunter will possibly have his limit in an hour or less. That is duck hunting and I wouldn't change it for anything.

People ask me what pleasure do I get out of duck hunting when I do not even eat duck. First, I really enjoy building a duck blind before season then it is the anticipation of opening date, setting decoys, putting on additional brush, then a fitful sleep through the night with anticipation of the opening morning. I also enjoy getting my retriever in top shape with afternoon exercise sessions. And then, it is opening morning and you are in the duck blind with the retriever and possibly a good hunting partner.

It's 30 minutes before legal shooting time now and the swamp is beginning to wake up. In the distance a hoot owl calls to another and to the east you can see the rosy hue, of coming sunrise. You cannot see good yet, but a mallard hen gives her wake up call. Then the whir of wings, still too early, but now it's time. You put your call to your mouth and get a pair to circle. They come in, good shot. The retriever does his job and with luck, you will limit out.

I also like to take pictures of the game I bag. And lastly, I enjoy giving a pair of mallards to a friend who really enjoys a duck dinner. This is _my_ pleasure, this is the pleasure I get out of hunting ducks.

15 BANDED DUCKS

I had mentioned previously about recovering 15 banded ducks. All these ducks were recovered in Louisiana.

This would be interesting to anyone to know a little about the three banded ducks I killed in one day. These ducks on my list are ducks # 9, # 10 and # 11. They were all recovered November 26, 1986 and they all were released from a different locations and on a different date. As the chart indicates, duck #9 came from Saskatchewan, Canada, duck #10 came from Laurel, Maryland, duck #11 from Manitoba, Canada. They didn't fly down to Louisiana together, but I bagged all of them the same morning. And I think that is very, very unusual, I've never heard of anyone doing that. Incidentally, I do have the newspaper clipping with this extraordinary feat of recovering three banded ducks on a legal hunt in one day. It was quite odd, like I said I've never heard of anyone else accomplishing that feat.

The following map notes each ducks migratory route. I have five from Canada and the rest are from the United States. It is interesting to see the way they funnel down to Louisiana, Of course I've stated before, some of the older birds had to fly great distances, if only back and forth. I think I previously noted that one of them would have to have flown 30,000 miles with no additional flying with the exception of getting to Louisiana and going back to its nesting ground.

I've hunted for over 60 years- most of it duck hunting. I've had my share of good luck. I also bagged a mallard muscovey hybrid which I had mounted and is now on my den wall. When the time comes when I can't hunt anymore, I'll have no regrets. I have enough memories to last a lifetime.

TYPE OF DUCK	DATE BANDED	WHERE BANDED	WHEN RECOVERED
1. Wood duck, male,	8/26/67	Columbia, Missouri	1/69
2. Mallard, male, adult	9/21/62	North Dakota	12/20/69
3. Mallard, male, adult	8/19/67	North Dakota	11/13/71
4. Gadwall male, adult	4/6/74	Springfield, Illinois	11/23/74
5. Mallard, female, 2 years old	2/15/76	Jackson, Mississsippi	1/9/79
6. mottled duck male, immature	7/31/79	Grand Chenier, LA	11/23/79
7. Mallard, male, immature	8/24/82	Laurel, MD	11/20/83
8. Mallard, male, mature	9/5/84	Columbia, SD	11/14/85
9. Mallard, male, adult	8/7/86	Saskatchewan, Canada	11/26/86
10. Mallard, male, adult	8/20/86	Laurel, MD	11/26/86
11. Mallard, male, adult	6/11/77	Manitoba, Canada	11/26/86
12. Mallard, male, adult	8/15/86	Manitoba, Canada	12/20/87
13. Mallard, male, adult	9/1/81	Saskatchewan, Canada	1/88
14. Mallard, male, adult	9/30/90	Stone Mills, New York	1/14/95
15. Mallard, male, adult	8/9/94	Saskatchewan Canada	11/30/95

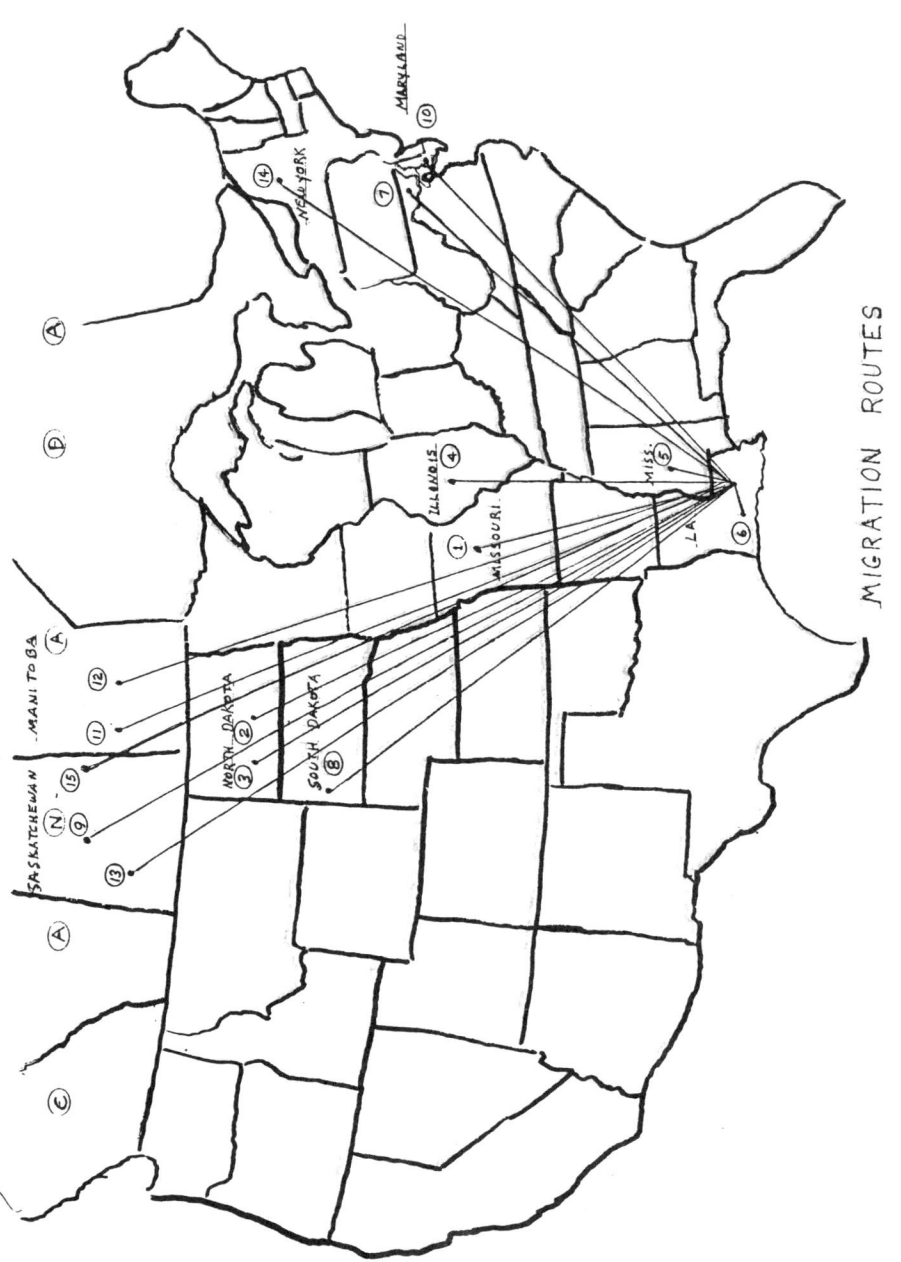

Hybrid Mallard - Muscovey duck bagged by the author.

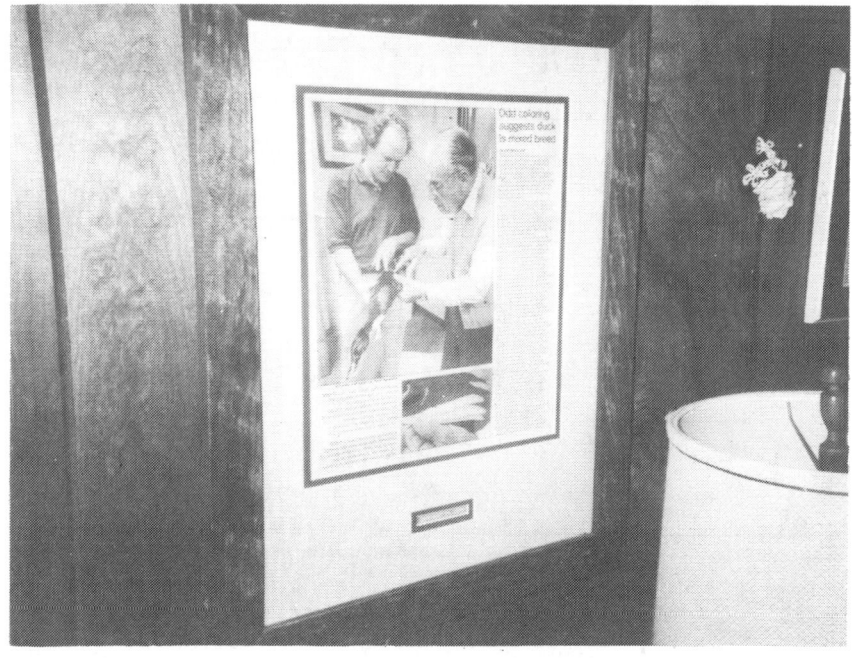

The author being interviewed by a Wildlife & Fisheries biologist on the hybrid mallard-muscovey duck.

My son-in-law, "Chet" and me with three banded mallards.

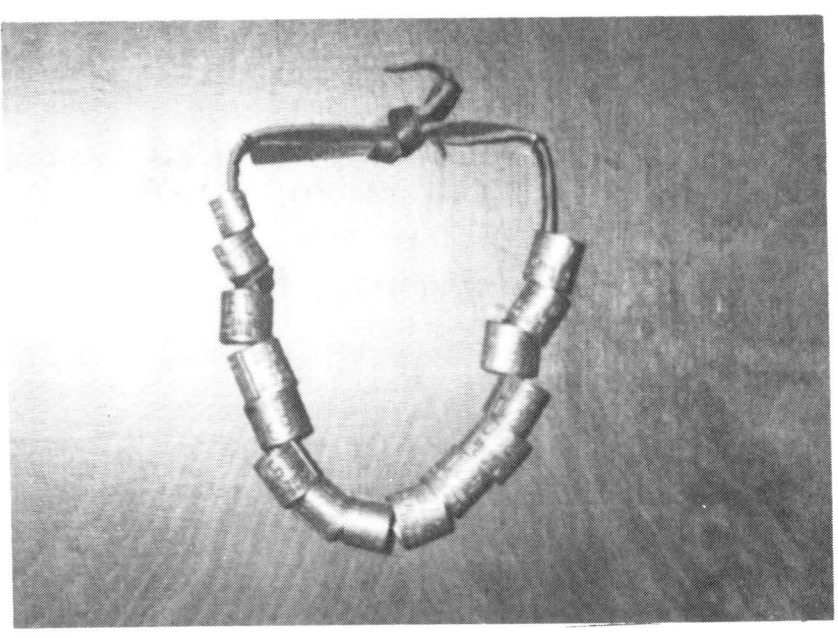

15 duck bands recovered by the author.

YOUNG AND FOOLISH

One Sunday afternoon while visiting with my wife's parents in Arnaudville, Louisiana, her father and I decided to go his camp on the Henderson levee. It was six miles to his camp and because of the rain, the levee was impassable. We decided to hook up the horse trailer and take his horse, Billy, so we could ride him to the camp. As the duck season was still open, we decided to bring his old pump shotgun.

It was a beautiful January day, clear but cold, but the sun was out and the cold was bearable. We motored to Henderson and unloaded the horse from the trailer and mounted up and were on our way. My father-in-law, George, in the saddle and me on the horse's back behind him with the shotgun across my lap.

We had covered about five miles when we saw a flight of dos gris fly up and then land ahead in the spillway. I told him I wanted to bag a couple of those ducks for his farm hands and he thought it was a good idea. Those ducks landed up ahead and swam near the bank and proceeded to feed. The bank where they landed was steep and I saw where I could approach them without being seen.

We rode the horse down the levee and I dismounted and proceeded to make my stalk. By staying low, I was able to get in range before they flushed. When they flushed, I knocked down two and they were belly up being carried downstream.

My father-in-law came riding up and asked me "How are you going to get them?" I told him I was going to swim out. With that, I ran down the bank in the direction they were drifting and began to take my clothes off. I stripped to my shorts and waded out about knee deep and it was just like standing in ice water. I told my father-in-law that the water is awfully cold, and he said, "Hit it all at once". So I did.

The farthest duck was about 100 feet away, so I decided to get that one first and get the other one as I swam back. When I reached that duck, I knew I had made a big mistake. It felt like a giant pair of arms was squeezing my chest. I let the duck go and started back to shore, but the current was very strong.

About half way back, I knew I was in trouble and I yelled for George to get the rope. I had seen him put a lasso in the saddle bag. He got the rope and waded out waist deep as I continued to try to get to shore. He threw the rope but it landed too short and I continued to struggle to get closer. I saw him coil the rope again, I was closer then, but the rope fell to one side. I continued to struggle.

The third time he threw, I caught the rope in the air and he drug me in like a log. I had a death hold on the rope. I crawled up on the bank, used my undershirt to dry off. I put on my clothes and he said, "Get on the horse and let's get to camp". I told him that I needed to walk. So he rode ahead and built a fire in the cast iron stove.

When I got there, after about a mile walk, he had a good fire going. The ride back was uneventful and I felt lucky to be alive. If I wouldn't have been young, about 24 years old and in good shape, I wouldn't be writing this today. That was more than 50 years and I vowed that I'd never be so stupid again. That's why I entitled this article "Young and Foolish."

"SIGHTS AND SOUNDS" OF THE SWAMPS

In a duck blind, I've watched a family of otters fish and play.

I've watched a king fisher catch a fish and kill it by beating it against a tree limb. I have had rosette spoon bills to wade among my teal decoys. I've watched an owl try to catch my top water lure. I've had on rare occasions watched a bald eagle and I've also seen fish eagles. I watched one time on Sunk Lake a peregrine falcon catch a duck and that was something to see. I've seen an osprey catch a fish and hold it in a streamline position as it flew to its nest. I've observed a great horn owl tend to two of its young in a cypress tree. I've seen pelicans feeding in a lake and observed one that had a two pound catfish lodged in his throat. I've seen, on several occasions, a dead cormorant hanging from a tree by a piece of fishing line that it had either had been entangled with around its neck or had eaten a live bait that the fisherman placed on the line. I was once hunting with my son and he bagged a mallard drake with one leg missing. I showed it to a local trapper and he told me that this happens often when a duck gets his leg in an animal trap.. In the spring, I've paddled into a night heron rookery and seen hundreds of nests with chicks to young to fly. I have seen a covey of quail scattered by a chicken hawk, also a robin knocked from the air by a kestrel. I've seen butcher bird catch insects and other small creatures and impale them on a barbed wire fence or thorn tree.

I've watched a spider come down a single strand of web, pick up a drop of water and bring it up with him and bring the web up, also.

I've snagged a small alligator on a bass bait.

Seen nutria scampering around the marsh, observed pelicans by the thousands fishing and also cormorants.

I've seen a mink trying to steal a duck that I'd shot that fell on the bank.

I've seen bass catch a frog, I've seen bass also kill a perch with his tail and turn around and eat it.

I've seen a mother raccoon guide her kits up a vine to feed on berries, a doe with her fawns, the countless rabbits and squirrels, multitudes of crows, red birds and buntings, in the fall the migration of the Monarch butterflies. I've seen balls of fire ants floating in the water, alligators sunning on the shore. I've listened at night to the sound of the swamp. A bull alligator bellowing, a coyote, owls calling to each other. Watched a wren build a nest, watched an armadillo dig for worms, and seen a deadly cotton-mouth and copperhead slither on the swamp floor.

I have caught bass on a fast moving lure that had only one eye. Also, bass with most of their tail missing and numerous times with different fins missing. I once caught a bass with a small mouse in his stomach. I have caught bass on a lure that never touched the water, the bass jumped up and took it off of a twig.

I've heard the squeal of a rabbit caught by a predator, also the sound of a frog caught by a snake.

The croaking of the bullfrogs at night.

This is what you see when you are hunting and fishing in the swamp.

NEAR DISASTER ON THE MISSISSIPPI RIVER

In the early 50's, I was working at a local refinery when my friend Bill, who was also an employee there asked me about making a duck hunt- He said, "Bud, how would you like to make a duck hunt at the mouth of the Mississippi?" I said, " I'd like to go, Bill, but how are we going to get there?" He said another one of our friends had a friend with a 21-foot cabin cruiser with a 50 HP motor on it. At the time, that was about the largest motor on the market, I'm talking about the early 50's. I said, "Count me in". So, the trip was planned.

We would leave Baton Rouge when I got off of work at 11:00 p.m. and drive through New Orleans to Venice, Louisiana, which is as far as you can go by car. This would be about a four hour drive as we would be pulling the big boat.

Well, we left Baton Rouge about 12 midnight, stopped in New Orleans for an early breakfast and gasoline, then finally got to Venice. When we stopped for gas, I asked the boat owner about gas for the boat. He informed me that his service station had filled both of his 12-gallon tanks.

At daylight, we launched the boat and proceeded down river to an area where the public is allowed to hunt. This was near the mouth of the Mississippi River which was down river about 15 or 20 miles. We had brought two pirogues along to hunt in the marsh. Half way to our destination, we passed the coast guard station which is about eight miles south of Venice.

Well, we got to the hunting grounds and we paired off, two to each pirogue and it didn't take long to get our limit. It was still early, and the boat owner suggested we do a little exploring so we went farther. After we got through exploring, we turned around and headed back upriver, and shortly, we ran out of gas in the first tank, but that was no problem as we had another tank.

It was starting to get late and we got just passed the coast guard station and ran out of gas in the second tank. Evidently, the station attendant had not filled the second tank. There we were, out of gas in the Mississippi River, with dark approaching and six miles to go to get to where our vehicles were parked at Venice. We tied up to a dead tree and tried to figure out what to do. With the fog setting in, I knew no one would see us. So, I suggested that two of us take a pirogue and paddle to Venice to get someone to bring gas to the cruiser.

Now you must know that the river is heavily traveled by ocean going vessels going to New Orleans and Baton Rouge. Jerry and I decided to paddle to Venice. We started paddling and soon it got dark and started to rain. We could not paddle close to the shore as the dead trees and logs come out in the river about 100 feet.

We figured we were about half way and it had gotten completely dark and we came to a party of hunters camped out on the shore. We could see their camp fire and Coleman lanterns and their three boats anchored out in the water.

Boats cannot be tied to the shore because of the wave action of the tankers going upstream and downstream. We pulled our pirogue up on the bank and walked to the camp sight about 50 yards on shore. They had three tents set up and a big fire going with ducks wrapped in foil in the hot ashes and they were eating steaks. We asked if they could spare a can of gas and they said they could and would bring us and the gas to our boat.

It was about 8:00 p.m. by then and we went to his boat and loaded the gas and shoved off. When we got on the river, the fog had thickened and we really had a hard time trying to follow the shoreline, as the trees, as I mentioned previously are out in the water.

After about an hour of hunting for our boat, we had to return to the camp sight as the fog had gotten bad. The hunter who seemed to be in charge said that we could spend a night with them; one of us in each tent. We thanked them and said that our friends would be worried, so we would take our chances and try to paddle to Venice.

One of the other hunters who had already gone to bed got up and said, "I'll find your boat for you". By the time he got dressed and got ready to go. like a miracle, the fog lifted. We got in his boat and you could see for miles on the river.

We went down the river looking for our boat, we couldn't find it. So this hunter took us to the coast guard station where we learned that our boat had been towed to port. The coast guard agreed to take us to Venice on one of its cutters.

Our friends were really relieved to see us. They thought that we had drowned. It was midnight and we got started back to Baton Rouge. We arrived at Baton Rouge at 5 00 a.m. That was two days without sleep!

RESCUE ON THE RED RIVER

This event happened in 1954 on the Red River above Simmesport, Louisiana. My father-in-law, George, and I planned a fishing trip to Sunk Lake where we had a camp. I had previously mentioned that I had a 25-HP motor, the largest made at that time and that I had built a plywood bateau This trip took place in mid March. We launched my boat at the landing called Three Rivers and proceeded up the Red River. There was a terrific current in the river and we had a strong south wind which made the waves higher than usual.

We were taking it real slow and easy, and about half way up the river near Grand Bay, we noticed a commercial fisherman in the middle of the river trying to paddle. The waves were breaking over this bateau as he was sitting on the bow, the boat had no motor on it. He had tried to run his catfish line across the river, but he didn't realize how rough the river was. I told George that I thought the man was in trouble. I motioned to him if he needed help, and he waved us over. I had to be real careful and not let my boat get in the trough, as we would have swamped also. I guided my boat along side of his boat and he jumped aboard still holding his bow line. The wave was so high that the bow of his boat came down on my motor and I had to tell him to let go of the bow line. When he did, I caught the bow line and his boat, by that time, was completely filled with water, but as it was made of cypress, it continued to float.

I began easing to shore and we pulled his boat on the bank and, believe it or not, all of his catfish were still in the boat. We even went out and caught his paddle and his bailing box. He began to cry and told us that we had saved his life. He offered us fish, but we told him we were only glad we could help and he owed us nothing. But he insisted we go up to his camp for coffee and that we should stop every time we came by if only to warm up on those cold days on the river.

We did a good deed that day and were justly rewarded as we later caught a tremendous string of black bass and we also made a good friend.

Sunk Lake lunkers.

ANOTHER OUTDOOR WATER SPORT

In the 1950's, I was coming back to Baton Rouge from "Grassy Lake", when I passed by False River. There was a boat race in progress, so I stopped and observed it for a while. I saw that there was a class for the same size motor as my 25 HP Evinrude. It was a stock class. Well, that got my attention. I proceeded to build a 13' runabout as that was the stock class.

At the refinery where I worked, I met Bill Lyon, who was a boat racer. He raced in the modified class. Bill and I became friends and decided to race as partners, concentrating on the stock class as that is what we could afford. We did all our own motor and propeller work, and started to have good luck.

We found out about the 100-mile marathons that were run at Greenville, and Vicksburg, Mississippi, in the Mississippi River, so we got involved.

Those events were big events in those towns and consequently, the idea spread to Yazoo City, Mississippi, for a 79 mile race on the Yazoo River, a 60 mile race on the Mississippi at Natchez, a 50 mile race at Monroe, LA, on the Ouachita River and several other long races, but the races at Vicksburg and Greenville were the big races.

Bill and I took turns winning some of these races and we always made enough money to cover our expenses. We also raced buoy races at different places,, such as Lake Charles, New Orleans, Ruston, and in the bayou country at Henderson, Port Barre and numerous other towns in Louisiana.

We always had the best class as we had the most entrants - as many as 20 to the heat.

In the big marathons, Bill and I would get there, each pulling our own boat, and those Mississippi boys would hate to see us arrive. We wouldn't do a lot of practicing so that they could see how we were running. We would simply put our boats in the water, but not crank up until race time, and we would usually beat them. We knew when we got there that our boats were ready as we would run them near Baton Rouge before "race day".

One time, on a deer hunt north of Vicksburg with those Mississippi boat racers, as we became good friends, I got the ultimate compliment from one of our competitors. We were in a large tent that held about 30 hunters and were in our sleeping bags on bails of hay and this fellow, who had a little too much to drink, said to me, "Bud, what in the devil are you doing to those motors? We cheat and still can't beat you all!"

That Mississippi race was quite an ordeal. 100 miles of Mississippi River, in a 13' runabout boat, on your knees, dodging river traffic, drift and all. It was quite a physical, as well as a mental achievement to win such an event.

Even though I raced boats for a few years, I never missed very many fishing trips or duck hunts.

I believe I have almost 40 trophies and plaques in my attic.

The author's race boat and trophies.

2 of the author's racing boats. At top, DeSilva racing runabout.

At bottom, Speedliner runabout

SAFETY

GUN SAFETY

The most important topic on hunting, I have to say, is safety. There are a lot of good rules such as never point a gun at anything you don't intend to shoot, but I've often wondered why more hunters are not killed when I see the way some people handle guns.

When you caution someone about carelessly pointing the muzzle of their gun in your direction, they will remark, "Well, the safety is on." Little do they know how easy a gun can be discharged with the safety on. With a small amount of trash or a seed or a piece of brush on the sear of the firing mechanism, a slight bump is all it takes.

I once saw a dog get in a boat and step on a gun and the gun discharged.

Never, ever have different gauge shotgun shell in the same shell vest or shell box, this is strictly a bad idea. You may in a moment of excitement put a small gauge shell into the magazine and then a catastrophe will probably happen.

When hunting with a partner in a blind or boat, have a firm understanding on whether to stay down or stand when it is time to shoot. Sadly, hunters have been killed when one stood and got shot in the head by his partner. I have seen shotgun barrels shot in two by the other hunter in the blind.

Another thing, never get in a boat without a life preserver on. I even use one in my pirogue, because really you have no chance of survival if you fall overboard with insulated clothes, a heavy hunting jacket and hip boots on.

And try to have a hunting partner with you, it is not a good idea to hunt alone. I'm guilty of this as I'm retired and usually hunt alone. If you have to, try to make someone aware of where you will hunt and when you expect to be back.

Another thing I like to mention is I believe it is a good idea to keep your unloaded shotgun in a gun case until you get to your blind. I have tripped and had the gun land in the mud, luckily it was in my gun case, as usual. A little mud in a gun barrel can have serious consequences - a blown barrel or possibly serious injury to you or your hunting partner. Keep your shotgun clean, if you do not know how to do this have a professional gun smith do it. An auto loader requires more cleaning and maintenance than other types. So bear in mind always keep your shotgun clean.

BOATING SAFETY

The next thing I want to touch on a little bit is boating and boating safety.

I have often wondered why there are not more accidents on the water than actually happen. I see people operating 200 HP boats and motors and that's the first boat that they have ever owned. They do not watch where they are going, they will turn the boat around without looking back, they have no regards for the damage that the wake makes.

I believe any newcomer who desires to purchase a boat should be required to take a water course.

The first large motor I had I purchased in 1953. It was a 1953 25 HP Evinrude Motor. It was the largest production motor on the market. Today that would be considered real small.

I have seen bass boats with as much as 260-HP motors on a 21" boat. The norm now is about 150 to 200-HP. And I know of one of the bass boats that clocked at 101.3 miles per hour on radar.

So, bear in mind when you're on the water, be cautious and watch out for the people with little experience.

The author with his boat and a two day limit of green heads.

ALCOHOL

I'd like to touch a little bit on the subject that affects a lot of people and that's alcohol. My saying is don't ever drink alcohol before or on a hunting or fishing trip.

Alcohol, as you know, is a depressant and will slow your reflexes, affect your eyesight, and also affect your equilibrium.

There is an old saying that gasoline and alcohol do not mix. Well, that goes for gun powder also; gunpowder and alcohol don't mix. If it is cold and you drink alcohol, you will get colder; if it is hot, you'll be hotter because alcohol will dehydrate you faster. Because alcohol is a diuretic, it will cause you to lose body fluids by excessive sweat and urination.

At the end of a day of hunting or fishing, when you are in your camp or home is the time, if you so desire, to have a drink. I have hunted with a partner once, who would bring a thermos of hot chocolate with him and I would bring a thermos of hot coffee; and we would share hot beverages in the blind, and that worked out real well.

I'd like to add, don't ever give alcohol to a person suffering from hypothermia; that will only worsen their condition. With a person suffering from hypothermia, you need to remove the wet clothes if they are wet and get them into some dry clothing and cover them with whatever clothing that you have available, a warm blanket and so forth.

For heat stroke, you need to get the person as cool as you can, give him water, water I'd imagine would be the best thing to give a person, that's what I would give him until you could get some medical attention. Also never give alcohol to a person who has a heat stroke. But in the field, you have to do the best you can - get a person warm who has been cold and also a person that has been overheated, try to cool them down with small amounts of cool water.

HAZARDOUS FISHING & HUNTING PLACES

Throughout the years, I've come across many excellent places to hunt and fish that were extremely hazardous places to navigate a boat. As I'm sure you understand, since these places were so good, we somehow overlooked the danger and did what was necessary to enjoy these spots. Here's a few I'd like to tell you about.

The first place that comes to mind is up on the Red River called "Sugar Mill Chute". "Sugar Mill Chute" drained a lake into the Red River. It would fill up in the Spring and would empty into the river in the Fall. It was a fantastic fishing spot, especially for top water lures.

When the river would "fall", it was really hazardous to negotiate going up or coming out of that chute. It wasn't too bad going against the current, as you could keep the power on your motor and go up as slowly as you desired, but coming out was a different matter.

The current coming out was at least 8 or 10 mph and there has been many boats capsize in that chute, with all the tackle falling in the water and getting swept out and lost. Most of the time, also the boat would be lost, as the current would lodge it against a log or tree and bend it in a "U" shape.

We used to take that chance because of the excellent fishing. Although we came pretty close to disaster many times, we never did capsize. Coming out in that strong current, we would not use the motor. We tried several times to use the motor in reverse, but that didn't work, so what we would do is have each person use a paddle, attempting to anticipate the twists and turns ahead and dodge obstructions, and <u>most</u> of the time, we did o.k. Once in a while, we would almost swamp, but we, somehow, managed to make it out o.k. It was a relief to finally get out into the river.

Next, I'd like to talk about "Lost Lake Chute". It is located on the Atchafalaya River and is another good fishing place. It is a chute similar to "Sugar Mill Chute", and also has a reputation for claiming a large number of boats, hunting gear and fishing tackle in its swift current.

One day, my old fishing partner, Mr. Mack, and I decided to make a trip to "Lost Lake" Now, "Lost Lake" is on an island, so you have to launch your boat in the river and go up this chute to get to the lake.

On this particular trip, we used a 12' bateau and a 6 HP motor because we figured we would have to portage around a small water fall. Sure enough, when we motored up the slough, we came to about a 2' water fall, so we unloaded the boat and portaged around the falls.

We fished until about 5:00 p.m. that evening and decided to head out, but instead of portaging, we decided to lower the boat down the little water fall by attaching 2 lines to the bow. Being that the water fall was not too wide at that point, having one man on each side with a line tied to the bow of the boat would make lowering the boat very simple - or so we thought!

Well, we were doing real good at first, but that current was really starting to exert a pretty good pressure. We would have been successful, however, my old partner, Mr. Mack, lost his footing, and away our boat went.

The boat filled with water and the gas tank broke loose from the motor and was being washed away. One tackle box was floating and the other had sunk. We ran down the bank and caught the gas tank, but the boat was lodged against a tree. We tried to get the boat free, but the current was exerting too much pressure against the boat.

Being on an island, we figured we would have to walk to the river and hope that someone would see us or we would have to spend the night in the swamp as no one else was on the lake at that late time of the day.

We began to try to figure a way to get that boat out. We were able to get the motor off of the boat and up on the bank. We then found a long pole, and by prying on one side of the boat, like a lever, we relieved some of the pressure off the boat and were then able to pull the boat up on the bank.

By this time, it was about 6:30 p.m., getting late. I then began to work on the motor. I took the spark plugs out of the motor and pulled it though several times to get the water out of the cylinders. We dried the plugs and connected the gas line, and when that little motor started, we were two happy men. We put it on the boat and started out, but noticed a lot of water coming in the boat, so we had to run the boat with the drain plug out.

When we finally got to the landing, I saw what was making the water come in the boat. The boat had a twist in it! If we would have had to leave it overnight in that current, it would have been completely destroyed.

When we got home, I told my partner to leave the boat with me and I would attempt to fix it. Sure enough, I straightened that boat and replaced 22 rivets that have been broken. It was as good as new!

We went back to the "Lost Lake Chute" the following week with a strong magnet in hopes of retrieving Mr. Mack's tackle box. This magnet was supposed to pick up 20 lbs. and since the tackle box was made of steel, we had a good chance of locating it.

We tied the magnet to a long pole and, as luck would have it, we caught the tackle box. This was, in fact, a good catch as his tackle box contained 2 expensive reels and about 50 lures. So much for "Lost Lake Chute".

The author with Sugar Mill Chute bass.

ODD HAPPENINGS

ODD CATCHES

Some things you just can't explain. I want to talk a little bit about odd instances that happened to me while I was bass fishing.

Several times, I've caught two bass on the same plug at the same time while fishing for bass. Most of the time, one bass would hit it and make a run, then evidently another one would try to take it away from him. But on these occasions, I was using plugs or crank bait, if you will, with two or three sets of treble hooks.

One time when I was fishing in some little trash willows that were sticking out of the water a foot or so and using a light spinner bait and reeling it rather rapidly, I had caught a bass about a pound and a half, maybe two pounds. Really, the fish weren't biting very good, so I fished down the bank of that impoundment, fishing from my boat. I made a cast and was coming through the little willow and I had a hit right on top of the water. I reeled in and there were two bass and the odd part about it was that this was on a spinner bait. Of course I had a trailer hook on the spinner bait but I find it real odd I could catch two fish on a spinner bait because it would be real difficult for both of them to get on, but they did.

I had heard of that happening way back when, a fellow that worked with me had told me about catching two bass at the same time on a spinner bait. That's real odd and I've talked to a number of bass fisherman and I can find no one else who ever remembered that happening.

Another time when I was fishing at one of the Ox Bow impoundments near Baton Rouge, I was fishing with a grub - a lead headed jig with a rubber tail on it - casting out, letting it go near the bottom and letting the current carry it, when I thought I had a strike. I started reeling and as I reeled in, up comes the tip of a rod! I reeled in a practically new rod and reel with about a two pound fish still on the line. So, evidently someone was fishing and hooked this fish, and the rod and reel fell out of their hand, and it had to be recently because the fish, about a two pounder, was still alive. I released the fish, brought the rod and reel home and cleaned it up and it was practically good as new, it was really an odd happening.

Another time I was fishing in the impoundment that had an out flow of water and there again ,I was using a jig with a rubber tail. I was fishing real slow, letting the current carry the lure, a single hook jig when I had a strike. When I set the hook, I had a tremendous battle, up and down he would take line. I would gain line back. There was another person standing there, I was standing on the bank, he was watching the fight. So, finally this person took my net and dipped up the fish, it was a 33 pound buffalo. I'd evidently drug the hook over the buffalo's back, and it hooked just in front of the dorsal fin and the odd part about this, two days later while I was fishing there for hybrid striped bass, the same thing happened again and I caught another 33 pound buffalo!

On each occasion, I gave it to the individual standing there, two different individuals, because they were real fond of that kind of fish, and I made them a present of it. I found it was very unusual to do that.

The author's son holding 2 bass caught at one time.

SPIKE'S BAY

One day, my friend, Bill, went fishing at "Spike's Bay". Now, "Spike's Bay" is a lake in the Atchafalaya Swamp and, when the water level dropped, was a fantastic fishing spot. Well, Bill and a friend went fishing and caught a limit of bass on that Thursday, while I was at work.

I stopped by Bill's shop and he told me they had made a good catch and also that a big bass broke his line. So, we planned a trip for Saturday. That morning, the weather was really cold. In fact, while waiting for the ferry at Bayou Sorrel, Bill had the truck radio on and it was announced that the temperature was 28°!

We bundled up and made that 5 or 6 mile boat ride and then, started fishing. I guess, we fished about an hour before we had our first strike, but then they really started to hit. The weather had warmed up a bit as it was a bright, sunny day, and the water was crystal clear. In fact, so clear that you could see a fish from the time it hit your bait until you landed it. I was using a spinner bait with a black skirt.

We finally came to the little slough where Bill said he had lost that big fish on Thursday. The little slough was about 8' wide. We fished the mouth of it and then continued on down the bank. We finally crossed to the other side of the little lake, as it wasn't but about 150' wide and continued to fish.

By this time, the sun was pretty high in the sky, so we crossed over so we could fish on the shady side. I made a cast by a stump and got a strike and, as I was reeling it in, I saw Bill's red & white lure in the fish's mouth!. I had landed the fish that had broke Bill's line on Thursday. I said, "Bill, this is that big fish that broke your line!" I know that the fish didn't weigh more than 2 lbs. - I guess Bill had a bad place in his line - but we sure had a good laugh.

A limit of Spike's Bay bass, caught by the author and Bill Lyon, my racing partner and fishing companion.

THE BIG ONE THAT GOT AWAY

I was fishing one day with one of my friends in a place called "Bayou Des Ourses". "Bayou Des Ourses" is in the Atchafalaya Basin. The mouth of this bayou has been plugged by the Corps of Engineers to keep silt from going into the Basin. In fact, they have plugged a lot of bayous for this purpose.

To fish this place, you had to launch your boat in the Atchafalaya River and bring a small boat also to portage over this plug at the mouth of the bayou.

On this trip, in fact, we had brought a pup tent as we expected to spend the night. We had never fished there before, but a friend at work had told us about the place and, sure enough, when we crossed the river, his boat was tied up, so we knew he was there also.

We started fishing and it must have been about 3:00 p.m. We continued to fish, but weren't having any luck. We came to a log jam, but saw a little opening that we could get through and around the jam. Still, we weren't catching any fish.

We fished on about another 300 yards and came to another log jam, which we went around in the same way. After we went around the jam, we spotted "Old Broussard" and his partner - then we started catching fish.

They were heading out in our direction, so we finally met. They had 2 stringers of fine bass and I told him that we had just started catching. He said, "I forgot to tell you to come pass the last log jam". I believe he forgot on purpose!.

I told him that he had some nice fish, but that I didn't notice any big ones. He said, "Boy, I lost a big one just a little while ago - he broke my line." I asked him what lure he was using and he told me it was a rainbow colored "Baby Dalton Special". Incidentally, we were catching all the fish on top water lures.

They left, paddling out, and we continued fishing. My friend decided to fly fish as those big "goggle eye" perch and bream were continuously trying to hit that top water plug.

He put on a small popping bug and started catching a few perch while I kept fishing for bass.

Our friend hadn't been gone 15 minutes when my friend had a strike on his popping bug and here comes the bass with the "Baby Dalton Special" in his mouth. We spent the night and fished the next morning and made a good catch.

The next work day, which was Monday, we brought that lure to our friend at work. We told him that the "big bass" couldn't have weighed more than 1½ pounds! His response was that probably 2 fish hit the lure at the same time or we just happened to find the lure floating!

We had a good laugh about that.

COULD HAVE BEEN WORSE

One afternoon, my son-in-law, Chet, and I decided to make a little fishing trip. I told him about a canal where we could catch a few bass, but we would have to pull a light boat over a dump. He said, "That is no problem, we will stop at Alcide's and borrow his little 10 feet bateau."

We launched my boat and proceeded to the Atchafalaya River where we stopped to borrow the little bateau. We loaded it across my boat and went a couple of miles to the Phillips' Canal.. There we tied up and pulled the little boat over the dump.

We had our fishing tackle, each had two rods and our tackle box. We started fishing and fished to the end of the canal, which took about an hour and at that time, we had seven nice bass.

We turned around and started fishing back. We were about half way back and, without warning, our little bateau was turned upside down and we found ourselves in the water!

I swam to the bank which was only about 30 feet away and so did Chet. He said to me in a very puzzled tone, "What happened"? I told him that the long snag overhead had just fallen on us. It was like a 20 ft. section of a telephone pole.

I realized that I had swam to the bank without letting go of my rod and reel! The little boat was upside down and three of our rods were under water and the two tackle boxes were floating. We found out that we could barely reach bottom, so we retrieved the boat and dumped the water out and by holding on to it and feeling with our feet found the other three rods.

That snag was about 10 inches in diameter and it missed Chet by about one foot and missed me by about three feet. It made a large dent in the side of that little boat.

I need to add that there was no wind blowing, it was just time for the snag to fall. We were very lucky not to have been severely injured or killed. Needless to say, that ended the fishing for that day.

AN ODD RETRIEVE

This is about a duck hunt that I made one morning with three of my co-workers. One of the fellows had a pretty large outboard cruiser, so we were able to, the four of us, to go in one boat. Before daylight, we put the boat in at a place called Blind River and proceeded to cross Lake Maurepas to the east shore.

When we got there, we tied the boat off and walked across a narrow strip of land to the edge of the marsh. We spread out along the tree line and began to try to get the mallards to pass over.

We had no decoys and no blind, but you had to have a retriever, a retriever was a must, as you could not walk to retrieve a duck if it fell past the tree line. But that was no problem, cause I had "Rusty", my retriever, with me. When it was legal shooting time, we started to get a few shots and were doing pretty good. One big drake came over and I made a high shot and he folded and fell through a tree and hit the ground. I sent Rusty to retrieve and, to my surprise, he came back with a headless mallard. I tried to figure out what had happened and the only thing I could conclude was that maybe I had shot that duck inadvertently with a buckshot. But after checking my hunting coat pocket, I found that the three buckshots that I carried in a special top pocket were still there.

The next thing I thought of was maybe a defective shell was used where there were several pellets that were matted together, but I could not come to any conclusion nor could any of the hunters. We all limited out and decided we had had such a good hunt, we'd go back the next morning.

Well, sure enough, the next morning we were in the same spot and I shot from where I was the day before. The ducks flew good that morning also, and we were about to limit out and, lo and behold, Rusty found the head of the duck that I'd shot the day before, a green head. Evidently, when that drake fell through the trees. The duck's head had caught in a forked branch and it was torn off. I told my friends, "now that's a dog, he couldn't bring me the whole duck yesterday, so he finished the job today".

HUMOROUS HAPPENINGS

NOTHING ELSE TO HOLD ON TO

This is pretty humorous although it was a little uncomfortable for one of our hunters on the trip.

We were hunting the marsh south of Morgan City near Point Au Fer. I was hunting with my partner, Cub, and "Saint" was hunting with his guest. Now, his guest wasn't really a seasoned hunter, but he was willing to try and old "Saint" invited him to make the hunt.

In the marsh, as you know, there is hardly anything to tie up to, so what we do is to attach an anchor to the end of our bow line and when you get to shore, just throw the anchor upon the bank. It was still about 30 minutes before daylight when we left the camp to make a hunt. We were in two boats.

We landed our boat at the canal bank with no problem, but there was far different happenings in the other boat. "Saint" told his partner, "When we get to the bank, step out and carry the anchor up the bank, then we'll get out and proceed to walk to the pirogues to make our hunt.

Well, old "Saint" cut the motor and was drifting to the bank and his friend stepped out, but he stepped out too soon, he went completely under and came up still holding the anchor!

Well, that called for a quick trip back to the camp for a change of clothes, as it was near freezing. After the hunt, we had a good laugh. "Saint" asked his friend why he had held onto the anchor. His friend replied, "I didn't have anything else to hold on to!" We really had a good laugh out of that.

INFLATING A MAE WEST LIFE PRESERVER TO SEE IF IT WORKS

Well, as you know, during the war there was a life preserver called the "Mae West" and so, this story is about that.

Four of my co-workers at Ethyl Corporation decided to make a squirrel hunt on the Red River north of Simmesport, LA. This required about a 10 mile boat trip. Mike was to supply the boat that he had won on a raffle for the trip. But not being able to swim, he was deathly afraid of the water. He proceeded to go to an Army surplus store and bought a "Mae West" life preserver.

Now, it got its name because of the way it is constructed. You have little CO_2 cylinders and when you squeeze the trigger mechanism, it inflates these tubes that are in the front of you on your chest, so that's the reason for the Mae West title for them.

They proceeded to go up Red River, loaded in the boat and old Mike was at the controls. So, he strapped on his "Mae West" and he said, "Well now I'm going to see if this thing works". Old Moore, one of our co-workers, said, " Mike, you're not supposed to inflate that thing until you fall overboard". He replied, "You must be crazy if you think I'm going to wait until I'm nearly drowned to try it out".

With that, he squeezed the mechanism and the two tubes inflated. The preserver was about to suffocate Mike when he yelled for help to get out of the preserver. They had a good laugh at that, but made the rest of the trip uneventful.

USING SPRAY PAINT AS MOSQUITO DOPE

This segment I thought was very funny and it involves my old hunting and fishing partner, Bill. Bill is an outboard mechanic.

Bill decided to make a rabbit hunt with one of his friends and so they loaded up in Bill's truck and drove several miles north of Baton Rouge to the woods that they were going to hunt.

When they got there, it was still way before daylight and they let the dogs out, as they were going to hunt with rabbit dogs.

The mosquitoes were real bad. So Bill's friend saw a spray can laying on the truck seat and began to spray himself, thinking it was mosquito dope. He said, "Hey Bill, is this mosquito dope supposed to be blue?" Bill said, "No. you fool, that's outboard paint". Bill had bought a can of Evinrude Blue because one of the motors he was repairing had to be repainted and he had left it on the seat of the truck. And his friend, thinking it was mosquito dope, had sprayed himself with Evinrude Blue. We thought that was very, very funny.

"BE SURE TO BRING THE PORK RIND..."

Years ago, before the fishing lures were equipped with the rubber skirts, most of the lures had buck tails of various colors. They used to say you have to put a piece of pork rind on that buck tail and that will give it a nice little flutter.

Back then, about the only pork rind that was available was in strips about three inches long and maybe a half inch wide. What you would do with that is you'd put it on the hook and it would enhance the appearance of the bait coming through the water especially if you reeled it kind of slow. It would ripple about like the rubber skirts do now. We're talking way back now, this is in the 30's.

So, my dad, a barber by trade, and one of his customers, who was just starting to fish, wanted to make a fishing trip with my dad. and my dad told him, "Why sure; I'll pick you up and I know a little stream that we can go to and paddle around and maybe catch a few green trouts". That is what they used to call bass then, "trout".

I believe I had mentioned before that some of the favorite lures were the shimmer wigglers and the shannon spinners which were buck tail lures.

But anyway, he told his customer, "Now, if you don't have any pork rind, pick up some because I think I have maybe one or two pieces and you might need some".

So sure enough, the next morning before daylight, my dad picked this man up. This man had his little rod and reel, a little small tackle box, and a paper bag with him. Well, my dad didn't think anything unusual about the bag - maybe the man was bringing a sandwich or two.

They proceeded to drive to the place where they were going to fish. Well, they got out and got the little boat in the water and started out. My dad put a piece of pork rind on the end of the lure and he asked the fellow if he brought some pork rinds. Well, the man opened the bag and took out about a two-pound piece of pork skin, that he had purchased at the butcher shop for his fishing trip. He wasn't aware of the little pork rind strips so he was doing what he thought was necessary by bringing about a two-pound slab of pork skin.

    My dad got him straightened out and gave him a little piece of pork rind out of his bottle. He went on and made the fishing trip and caught a few bass, as well as received an education about fishing with pork rind.

UPSIDE DOWN LONG JOHNS

As you know, you wear "long johns" when it is cold because they are really comfortable. Now, most everybody has the two-piece "long johns". I guess a few people still use the long one piece kind, but not many that I know of. But anyway, this was on one of those jellybean hunts that I talked about previously which I arranged.

We were down at one of the hunting clubs in southwest Louisiana. We had a bunch of clients down there, who mostly were occasional hunters. Several of the fellows, decided they would play cards that night. Well, most of us turned in around 10 o'clock, but there were three or four fellows that decided to just go ahead and keep playing cards all night long, and since they were guests, I more or less let them do what they wanted to do. They had a few beers and they played cards until it was time to leave the camp the next morning to make the hunt.

Well, when morning came and it was time to make the hunt, they went into the back room and retrieved their hunting clothes, insulated clothes and whatever, because it was pretty cold that morning. They dressed and we went on and made the hunt. When we got back, one of the fellows that probably had a beer or two; too many, with no sleep, started to put on his clothes to travel back to Baton Rouge. He discovered that he had put the long john top on his legs! The rest of the fellows there couldn't believe their eyes.

I'm telling you it was hilarious to see him undressing and to see the top half of his long johns on his bottom half! Now we don't know how he managed to relieve himself or nothing else, but that's a fact and that gave the whole crew a real good laugh.

The several guys that drank a few too many beers and played cards all night spent most of their time sleeping in the blind and the rest of the hunters had a real good hunt. So that's the price they had to pay for having their fun the night before.

"I'M GLAD YOU DIDN'T KILL THAT DEER!"

I want to talk about old Alcide my swamp friend, who had virtually spent his entire life in the swamp.

He was telling me about a deer hunt that he went on and how it was done. There would be maybe a dozen hunters and they'd pick a spot in the swamp and stretch out a stand line. That is with hunters more or less in a line separated by enough distance where you couldn't possibly shoot one another.

Then the deer driver takes the pack of dogs and goes up from the stand line about a couple of miles and releases the dogs and urges them on towards the stand line, in hopes they will jump a deer and run it through the stand line and maybe someone will get a shot.

Well, sure enough, they did this and had everybody in place and the driver released the dogs. The dogs circled around awhile and finally hit a trail and started barking and running the deer. Sure enough, the deer headed south because the driver had gone north because they know the deer is going to run into the wind where he can smell if there is trouble ahead. They had planned it correctly and the dogs were running the deer and after a good long chase, sure enough, the deer came through the stand line.

One of the hunters got a shot. Well, when the dogs got there to the stand line, everybody converged on the hunter who had fired the shot to see if he needed help to pull the deer out. He was exclaiming to them that it was a tremendous buck and he had shot it and he knew that he had hit it, but it didn't stop.

They began to look for maybe a blood trail or hair or some sign of a crippled deer, but didn't find any sign of a crippled deer. So they came back to the spot where the man did the shooting and they asked him "Now, where was the deer when you fired the shot?". He said, "He was over in that direction and I know I had the gun right on him, I shot him and I know I hit".

Well they looked around and my friend, Alcide, looked up about eight feet up on a big oak tree and there was the whole load of buck shots. So he told the hunter, "You know, I'm glad that you didn't kill that deer because if you had your gun right on him and he was that big, we would have had to gone back and gotten a tractor or team of mules to pull that deer out because as big as he would have been, we certainly couldn't have pulled him out with just man power!

Everybody had a tremendous laugh about that and that hunter got kidded about that for a very long time. That was a tale old Alcide enjoyed telling and it always drew a big laugh from whomever he told.

"LOUIS' DUCK HUNT - A BROKEN GUN."

One of my friends of long ago told me of a duck hunt he made in the Manchac Swamp.

It seems that he and his partner were scouting the swamp for a duck roost. They each had a single barrel shotgun. Well, about sundown they saw a place where the wood ducks were pouring in. My friend Lewis told his buddy not to shoot as they would only scare the ducks because the single barrel shotguns would be of little use when the ducks were coming in that thick. He told his friend of a plan. He said, "Let's go to town and borrow a couple of automatics from a friend that has them, and like that, when we come back tomorrow afternoon, we will have five shells to shoot before we have to reload".

Sure enough, the next morning they both borrowed automatic shotguns. The lenders showed Louis how to load the guns.

That afternoon they proceeded to go to the swamp to wait for sundown to shoot the duck roost. As sundown approached, each loaded their guns and waded out knee deep in the water, they took up a stand about 75 yards apart. Well, as it began to get near sundown, the ducks started to pour in and the hunters started shooting. After Louis' fifth shot, the breech block on the automatic stayed open and Louis thought a piece of the gun had fallen into the water. In fact, he thought he heard it hit the water. Actually, it was the last empty case that he had heard. This was during "the Depression" and Louis didn't know what he would do if he broke the man's gun.

He was afraid to move, so he kept his feet in the same spot while reaching under water feeling for the lost piece of the gun, all the while calling for his friend to come and help him. His friend was too busy shooting to come and see what was the matter.

So, well after dark, his friend finally came and poor old Louis was about to freeze, his feet still in the same spot and he was still feeling under the water! His friend asked Louis what was wrong and Louis explained his plight. At that, the friend said, "Let me see the gun". Louis handed him the gun and his friend pushed the button to close the action and the gun was fixed!

Louis told me he would never again borrow a gun he was not familiar with. He was a good sport and laughed at his own ignorance.

MR. MACK'S QUAIL HUNT

I just thought of a story about my old friend, Mr. Mack, when he lived as a young man in North Carolina near Winston-Salem that I know will be interesting to whoever hears it. In that part of the country at that time, quail were plentiful. You could ride through the countryside and stop at a farmer's house and ask permission to make a hunt and more than likely, he'd let you hunt. He'd also tell you where you might find a few covey of quail, So, Mr. Mack and one of his friends took off one day and they just did that.

They drove through the countryside and came to a likely looking spot and the owner, the farmer, was out front, so they stopped and inquired. He said, "Yes y'all can make a hunt, I'd be glad for y'all to make a hunt, there are a lot of birds back there, I see them all the time and I hunt them myself once in a while".

So, they got out of the car. Mr. Mack let his two high powered bird dogs out. They were real fine bird dogs. One of them was named, "Greek" and I don't remember the name of the other. But they were so highly thought of that he had an oil painting of these two dogs, and I imagine that his widow still has the painting. So they were really something.

Well, they got the guns out of the car and started to walk across the barn yard and the old farmer called out to them, he said " Look, do y'all mind if I come along?" "Oh no...", they said, "We'd be real glad to have you". So he got his gun also and they started to walk and when they passed the barn, a straggly-looking pointer came out and wanted to follow along. The farmer scolded him to go on- get back.

They proceeded to walk another 50 yards and the dog tried to follow again. Well, the farmer picked up a clod of dirt to throw at him like he was going to hurt him and told him to go on back now. So my friend Mr. Mack says, "Well look, let him come, will he point a bird?" And the fellow says, "Yes, I use him quite a bit, but I didn't want him to interfere with your dogs".

Mr. Mack told the farmer that the old dog wouldn't interfere with his dogs, .and to let him come on. Well sure enough, they went on and hunted, and to make a long story short, Mr. Mack told me that they found eight coveys of quail and every covey that was found, those high powered dogs were backing that little straggly pointer! That pointer found every covey and the way Mr. Mack put it, he said, "By dog ,every time we'd come up to where they were pointing, my two dogs were looking straight up his behind, he had those birds nailed down". So evidently, that dog knew the ranges where those birds used and that's why he was able to find them ahead of Mr. Mack's dogs. And Mr. Mack got a big chuckle out of that because his dogs were real fine. But that little country pointer put it on them that day.

Along the same lines, I had a bird dog, a liver and white pointer, that my father-in-law, George, Kept for me at his home in Cecelia, LA.

One day, a couple of business men from Lafayette, LA, were passing and they saw George out front with my dog so they stopped.

They were looking for a place where maybe they could make a hunt as they also had their dogs in the car. They inquired of George if he knew where they may find a covey or two of quail. Here the similarity of the story seems almost fictional.

George told them that he had nothing to do and would gladly show them a place across the road where they might have some luck.

The two men got out of the car and let their dogs out. Goerge got his gun and shells and, with my dog, crossed the road and went into the fields.

It wasn't long before my dog was on point and those men got to bag a pair of quail.

They went on and pretty soon my dog was on point while the men's dogs were backing my dog.

They found several coveys that afternoon and it was the same scenario as with Mr. Mack's dog. The men raved about the way my dog ranged and worked the fields. When they finished the hunt, they inquired if my dog was for sale. George told them "definitely not". They got my address in Baton Rouge and sent me a real fine complimentary letter in regards to my dog, stating that if I ever decided to sell him to let them know. They added that they would be willing to pay a handsome price!

I kept the letter for a long time as a testimonial to my dog. Of course, I never responded to their offer. As I have said before, quail hunting was a big thing for me until I got into duck hunting and further, until quail got scarce in that area and I decided to concentrate on ducks. Even though that was many, many years ago, I still remember the thrill of a covey rise and the beautiful work of a good pair of bird dogs.

CANADIAN "GOOSE" FEVER

I want to relate an event that happened in the 1950's to a friend and his hunting partner - both experienced duck hunters.

They were hunting ducks in the Atchafalaya Basin, in the arm of "Grand Lake", where they had built a duck blind. It was well up in the morning and the duck action had slowed down.

They looked up and four huge Canadian honkers were circling to land. They landed on the south end of the lake and began feeding. The wind was out of the north, so my friend thought he could sneak up on them.

He asked his friend if he had some magnum loads of No. 2's and his friend said that he did. He loaded his old '97 model Winchester up with three shells, cut a load of brush and piled it in the front of the pirogue.

He started his sneak attack, crouching low in the pirogue (at the time, sneaking was not illegal). He was doing pretty good - the wind was taking him directly to the feeding geese. When he got in range, he raised up and the geese took off, flying into the wind. They passed directly over him!

He unloaded all three shells, but he forgot to pull the trigger. That is "goose fever".

UNCLE ALCIDE'S "TALK" WITH HIS DOG

One day, I got to my camp about mid-morning and when I landed my boat, I was greeted by the familiar words, "Come on up, I have a fresh pot of coffee on the stove".

I unloaded my gear at my camp and went over for a cup of coffee and a "made from scratch" hot biscuit. I had brought him, as usual, a Baton Rouge newspaper. We talked for a while.

I finally went to my camp which was about 150' from Uncle Alcide's trailer. Uncle Alcide's trailer was a 14' x 70' house trailer that was hauled to its location after the 1973 flood. His brother who was in the oil filed business hired a tug and a barge plus the bulldozer and manpower to get it where it is.

After the land was cleared and the trailer hauled ashore and put on supports, Uncle Alcide installed 2 porches, one on the side which was 8' x 20' and one on the back which was 8' x 12'. Each porch had a swing and several chairs. It was a real fine home with butane lights and stove, plus, at a later date, solar power. For a long time, he used a generator, but with solar power, he stopped using the generator. It had 2 bedrooms and a den, kitchen and bath - a real nice setup.

I started doing a few chores and, after a while, I could hear Uncle Alcide talking to someone. He had a high-pitched voice and it was easy to hear him. I thought, "that's funny, I didn't hear anyone motor up". (That is the only way to get to the camp).

I listened a while longer and finally, my curiosity got the best of me. I decided that I had to see with whom he was talking. At this point, I could only hear his voice.

I eased over to his place and found him mending a hoop net. He was describing every movement to his dog, "Black Boy" (he called him "Black Boy" even though he was black and white). He didn't see me approach, so I left as quietly as I came, so he would not be embarrassed.

I guess, in later years, when the amount of his company declined, he had to have "someone" to talk to and seemingly "Black Boy" filled the bill just fine.

I know that he talked to "Black Boy" as he would a human being, for one day, "Black Boy" had chased Alcide's cat. Alcide asked me, "Bud, is that dog chasing the cat?" I confirmed that he was. Uncle Alcide then informed me, "I told him yesterday to leave that cat alone or I'd tan his hide. I guess he forgot that I told him."

Uncle Alcide's Dog, "Black Boy".

The Old Swamper, "UncleAlcide" Verret, holding a big bass caught by the author.

ALARM CLOCK SNAFU

The night before the opening of the second split of the duck season, I went to bed, full of anticipation, as I had seen lots of ducks when I went out to the blind to set decoys and touch up the brush. After tossing and turning, I finally fell asleep, but it was a fretful sleep as the expectations of the next morning would not let me relax.

After waking up several times, I finally decided to turn on my night light and look at that "Baby Ben" I kept on my night stand. When I looked at the clock, it was 4 o'clock, as I had it set for 4:15. I said to myself, "Well, I just as soon get up now".

As usual, I put my coffee water on the stove and began to build a fire in the cast iron heater. I got it going pretty good, lit the other burner on my gas stove to heat my cast iron pot to make biscuits. My coffee water got hot and I began to drip my coffee. Well, pretty soon the coffee was made and I had my first cup. Now, I had to wait on my biscuits.

I looked at the clock again and it was 1:00 a.m. - I couldn't believe it, so I looked at my wristwatch, and sure enough, 1:00 a.m. I had misread the clock and actually when I thought it was 4 o'clock, it was 12:20 a.m.! I had made a mistake between the little hand and the big hand!

Well it was no way to go back to steep, as I had drank coffee and the adrenaline had started to flow. I ate my biscuits and whiled away about four hours reading old newspapers I had at the camp that I always brought to start a fire.

What a snafu, but I did read some news that I missed when the paper was current. In spite of this, I had a good hunt that day, but needless to say, I had to take a nap when I got in from the hunt!

CAMPING

MY CAMPING BOX

Years ago, when I used to do a lot of "roughing it" camping, I found the need for a portable camp box that would hold the essentials for an overnight camping trip, so therefore, I designed and built a box.

The box was made of 3/8" exterior plywood, with overall dimensions being 20" wide, 24" long and 18" high.

Earlier I described George's camp box, but I made mine more compact so that I could carry it in my bateau.

The lid was not hinged, but would fit over the box and had a 2" lip on it so it was literally rain proof. I installed 2 quite large fold down handles so that 2 people could get a good grip on them. I have handled the box occasionally by myself, but would unload the contents first.

Even though it was not susceptible to being blown off, I installed a suitcase latch on 2 sides.

Inside the box, I carried 2 Coleman lanterns, a one-burner camp stove, a skillet, a small coffee pot, a pan for boiling water, a 4 quart pressure pot, eating utensils, Coleman fuel, a flash light, matches, paper plates, coffee cups, plastic drinking glasses, and staples such as plastic airtight containers of coffee, sugar, rice, cornmeal, cooking oil, salt and pepper. These items stay in the box the entire season. I need to add, I also had a 3-sided wind shield for the cook stove so that the wind would not blow the flames of the Coleman stove.

When we were ready to go camping, we would add a couple of potatoes and ½ dozen eggs. We also carried the bread in this box so that it would not get mashed. You know mashed bread will never straighten out.

We would load our box in the truck, along with a pup tent and our sleeping bags and take off. We would launch the boat and begin hunting or fishing with no definite plans on where we would camp. When it got to be late afternoon, we would start looking for a spot to camp.

When we found a spot, we would off-load everything and set up camp. We used the camp box as a counter top to cook on and after that, we would use it as a table to eat on with a couple of boat cushions as "chairs". That always worked out pretty good.

I forgot to mention that in the box I marked off with a marker where everything went because if not, you would have trouble fitting everything in.

I know a box of this kind will help you guys and gals who like to "rough it" once in a while.

The author's camping box.

CAMP AND "LEAN TO" BUILDING

In 1947, after returning from over-seas Army duty, my father-in-law, George, and I built a camp on the levee, about 6 miles north of Henderson, LA. We hunted out of that camp for several seasons and did pretty good, but the camp was always plagued by vandals, so we had to look for another place.

In 1949, we went up on the Red River and found a very primitive little shack owned by a local fisherman. You could stand on the outside and see someone on the other side of the camp.

We went up there with 3 rolls of tar paper and completely wrapped it with the tar paper. We then cut out the windows with our pocket knives.

Inside was an old iron stove and an old table. The shack was about 12' x 20' and it was quite airy. We hauled an old bed and a single cot there. The three of us, George, Mr. Mack and me, spent several duck seasons there.

The duck hunting and bass fishing was fantastic until the lake was leased to an individual and we had to give it up.

It's funny how things come and go. You find a place to hunt or fish and, pretty soon, it goes by the wayside for one reason or another.

After losing our place on Sunk Lake, we found a good place on the Arm of Grand Lake below the Amarada Pumping Station. Every year, we would put up a "lean to" or cook fly, if you will, and while I'm on the subject, I'll describe how we installed it.

We would find 2 trees about 20' apart, nail a pole from one tree to the other, and place a pole about midways between the two trees. We had a canvas tarp, 18' x 18', and we would put it over the pole, letting the side come to the ground on the north side and, on the south side, we would let it extend, like a porch. We would use poles and guy ropes to keep it extended. That's where we did our cooking on a homemade table from local timber. We had a fine little 8' x 10' tent with screen windows and a zipper door with a sewn-in bottom, which worked real good. We slept on Army cots and had 3 Coleman lanterns, a Coleman heater and a Coleman stove. We hunted out of this set-up for about 3 years, and then, the water hyacinths took over the lake in which we were hunting. This was in the 1960's.

When this ended, I had the good fortune to get to hunt below Morgan City, LA, which I have described previously. When that played out - as I said before, it seems that everything comes to and end - it was back to the Atchafalaya Swamp, another lean-to, the same tent, and the same set-up. I have pictures of both set-ups, and even though they are about 10 years apart, you can't tell the difference.

The author cooking breakfast after the hunt.

The author and Mr. Mack Markland with a limit of mallards form an arm of Grand Lake, below the Amarada Pumping Station.

CAMP CHORES

Even though I go to my camp every week, there is a special urgency prior to the opening of duck season and that is, checking the pirogues for any bad spots, repainting when necessary, touching up the camouflaging, and sanding and repainting the paddles, replacing the bow lines and so forth.

Next is the decoys, touching up the paint if necessary, giving them a good cleaning in a tub of water and detergent, replacing anchor lines and weights if necessary,

Then it's cleaning and clearing the trails through the woods, checking the water levels to see where to put the blinds and hauling the pirogues through the woods.

And now it is time to start gathering fire wood. I go down the canal from my camp and try to find an ash tree. It's the type of wood I like to get because it's easy to split and it burns easily. When I find a suitable tree, not too far from the canal, I cut it down with my chain saw, then I cut it into about 18 inch chunks and haul it to the canal bank and put it in my boat. Then to the camp and up the hill to be split. I like to cut it in September, although it is usually hot, but I like to cut it soon enough so that it will be good and dry for November.

Then it is work on the camp, if necessary - fixing the screens, nailing down a loose piece of roofing, etc.

Every fall, I spray insecticide under the camp to discourage insects and snakes, rake all the leaves away from the camp to prevent a fire.

Next, I clean the stove and the stove pipe, and check the stove pipe for leaks and replace, if necessary.

About two weeks before opening day, it is time to start on the blind and brush them so the brush won't look too new. And also, if early ducks arrive, they will be used to the blind.

Then I take inventory of my supplies and stock up on extra provisions like staples, coffee, sugar, flour, cornmeal, potatoes, onions, cooking oil, a case of cold drinks and emergency foods like pork and beans, soup, chili, corn, peas, hot chocolate mix, granola bars, mosquito dope, charcoal lighter, extra batteries and so forth. The food items are for use when I don't feel like cooking.

I also should add along with the provisions I've mentioned, an important consideration is having extra clothes - extra pants, shirts, socks, heavy and light underwear, extra boots, extra rain gear, extra gloves and hunting caps. It is real comforting to know especially when you get wet, that when you get back to the camp, you can dry off and have nice dry clothes to put on.

I try not to forget anything as it is a 10 mile boat ride back to the landing. I also bring in extra gasoline and oil.

All this should be done a couple of weeks before opening day.

The author's camp in the Atchafalaya Basin.

Guy Allen bush hogging a trail to the lake.

The author using a ditch bank blade to cut the overhang.

A good "lean to" and tent set up.

WORST CAMPING SETUP

I am going to relate what I call one of the worst setups I ever saw of three people who were setup on Grand Lake where we had our little tent and cook fly which I have described previously.

It was about maybe 2 or 3 o'clock in the afternoon and here comes a bateau boat with an older man in it, who I later found out was 75 years old and his two sons. They pulled up on the bank of this canal or bayou about 50 yards below where we were set up and proceeded to unload some stuff. Evidently, they were going to make a duck hunt because this was the season. Well, we were set up beautifully where we were, had all the conveniences that we needed and I kept watching these fellows get their stuff together, just before dusk one of the sons, I guess the man was maybe 35 or 40 years old, came walking to our set up. He had a new Coleman two-burner lantern in his hand and he walked up and he said, "Do you fellows know anything about a Coleman lantern?" I said, "Yes, we have three right now that we're getting ready to fire up". "I don't know how to light this lantern,", he said, "it's new and I can't seem to get it lit." He had filled it up with gas, but didn't know you had to pump up the tank.

So, we walked back over there with him to their set up, I pumped up the tank and put a match to the mantle and away it went, it was glowing beautifully. He thanked us very much. So then I saw how they were going to sleep and I was amazed, I've never seen that before. The father and his sons had put a sash card tied between two trees, the trees were about 12 feet apart, and this piece of sash card, you know it's about a 3/8-inch rope, was tied about 2 feet off the ground from one tree to the other. They had a new tarp, I can tell you it looked like a brand new tarp. What they did, if you can picture this, was put half of the tarp on the ground under the rope and the other half of the tarp over the rope. I know it wasn't more than 2 feet off the ground or less and the older man, as it was almost dark by that time, had already crawled under there to go to sleep and the two sons were about to do the same thing.

We were able to observe that all of them went under there and spent the night -the three men -with all of their clothes on. The next morning, they got up about the same time we did, an hour or so before daylight. I saw them fire up the Coleman lantern, they had learned how, and they also made a duck hunt. That's about as primitive as I've ever seen.

WORST CAMPING TRIP

I believe the worst camping trip I ever went on was in 1950. It was suppose to be a duck hunt on Sunk Lake. It was planned with my father-in-law and two co-workers when I worked at a local refinery.

As I've said previously, Sunk Lake is on Red River. We had never been there, but one of the co-workers had some relatives that lived in the area. The nearest town was Simmesport, and the way I remember, we were to leave Baton Rouge, the four of us in my car, and we were going to drive to Simmesport.

When we got to Simmesport, we were to have a "guide", and I'll use that term lightly, because it was just a relative of one of my co-workers. He was going to provide transportation to the lake. The lake is 15 miles up the Red River. The only thing we were going to do to, more or less, to compensate the "guide", was to bring a couple fifths of liquor and a gallon of wine which we did. We didn't partake in any of that, but those "guides" had a good time with it.

We left Baton Rouge at an early hour and arrived at Simmesport at around 9:00 a.m. because we were going to spend a night. When we got to Simmesport and located our "guide", there was no transportation available. So, after an hour or so, we finally got a local fisherman to agree to bring us to Sunk Lake. We were five men in a 14 ft. boat with the fisherman with a 10-horse motor, if you can imagine that. The trip took three hours, - that's <u>three hours</u> for 15 miles - before we arrived at Sunk Lake. We had been told that at Sunk Lake the local fishermen would have nets full of sac-a-lait , that's another name for white perch.

All we had to bring was bacon, corn meal, cooking oil, salt and pepper, and bread. We'd have fried fish and then we would duck hunt and bring ducks home. We weren't supposed to cook any duck because we didn't bring any cooking facilities.

When we finally got to Sunk Lake, there were no fish available to eat and really, no sleeping quarters. We had each brought a bed roll, but no shelter. There was an old abandoned shack, that I had talked about previously, that we eventually made into some kind of living quarters by encasing it in tar paper - it was located there.

We threw our bed rolls on the floor and agreed that these arrangements would have to do for that night. It was just an open structure that had a roof over it - not very substantial. We just hoped that it wouldn't rain.

We went out to the lake, had a couple of old skiffs there, paddled out to some existing duck blinds, and prepared to make a duck hunt that afternoon. We did make a duck hunt, we killed several ducks. The lake was covered with poule d'eau also. Some of the fellows shot some of the poule d'eau because they have a large gizzard and some people like to eat poule d'eau gizzards.

After the hunt, at just about dark, we went back to the sleeping quarters if you will, this tiny place with no provision to sleep on- just the floor.

One of my co-workers borrowed a pot from the fisherman that lived several hundred yards from where we were, made a bonfire, put oil in the pot and proceeded to cook poule d'eau gizzards. I wasn't about to eat poule d'eau gizzards. I could see while he was cooking and stirring the pot over that open fire. A lot of flying insects were around and I think a lot of them were going in the pot! I told one of my other friends and my father-in-law that I'm was not going to eat any poule d'eau.

So, I got out the pound of bacon we'd brought and I got a little forked stick and I roasted some bacon like a wiener roast and I put bacon, half cooked. between slices of bread and ate that. One of my co-workers didn't want any poule d'eau gizzards either, so he also made himself a bacon "sandwich", but we were still hungry. He said, "Man I'm so hungry I'm getting a headache" I said, "Look, let me show you a trick." I took two slices of bread and put sugar in between and made a sugar sandwich, and he did the same.

I've got to laugh now, thinking back on this - the fellow's name was "Moore", and he said, "You saved my life because after I ate that sugar sandwich my headache went away and I was like a new person".

Well, we spent a night under those conditions, went out the next morning and killed a couple more ducks. I need to add the reason this other friend wanted to cook the poule deau gizzards - he wanted to bring some ducks home to show his wife and his neighbors that we really succeeded in killing some ducks.

So, at the end of the hunt the next day, there were several more local fisherman on the river and we split up the load and we came down the river in several boats instead of just one. We made it back about half the time.

That was really a pitiful trip as far as I'm concerned.

THE THREE "UNWISE" MEN

This is a true story about a camping trip in the Atchafalaya Basin about my son, Richard and his two companions from Texas, Curtis Burch, a pharmacist and Tom McCorkel, an insurance agent.

Every year in the Fall, Tom and Curtis make their pilgrimage to Louisiana, to venture into the wilderness of this great basin. They prefer to go to some isolated spot to "get away from it all" for a 3 night camp out.

It was about 7 p.m. when they stopped by my house in Baton Rouge to tell me they were heading out. The bed of the pickup truck was loaded with a tent, sleeping bags, and everything necessary for the outing, and they were pulling Richard's 14' bateau with the 20 HP Mercury motor. I wondered if the boat would float with three big men aboard and all that equipment!

I told them they should wait for the morning as the weather was pretty bad and that thunder storms were predicted for later that night. They didn't want to lose a night of camping out, so they chose not to heed my warning. I said, "Well, tell me about where you are going and I'll check on you all tomorrow". Richard said, We are going down the river to that pipe line crossing - that site is always pretty clean and we won't have to clear much brush."

Curtis is the "cook" on these outings and he comes up with some pretty good meals, he even cooks a roast over an open fire. Tom is the ordinance expert. He always brings several guns and a good supply of ammo for his target practice. Richard is the "guide".

I insisted they take my new 14' canvas tarp to cover their supplies, as they only had a small dome tent to sleep in. Incidentally, their trip by boat is approximately 12 miles, with part of the trip in the Atchafalaya River.

Well, soon after they left Baton Rouge, the weather began to get really bad and I began to worry about them. I had a fitful night's sleep and could hardly wait for daylight to hook up my boat and go to check on them.

The weather the next morning broke and it was a beautiful day. I hooked up my boat and was on the way. I launched my boat and fired up my 140 HP Johnson and headed my Allison bass boat to the spot where I knew they would be.

When I spotted their campsite, it looked like a disaster area! They had a rope stretched between two trees and were attempting to dry out their belongings - luckily, the sun was shining!

They began to relate to me the events of the trip. They launched the boat and loaded the camping gear aboard, and as I had assumed, they had only about 3 inches of "free board". That 12 mile trip took over 2 hours, and as they made their way, the weather got worse!

When they got to the Atchafalaya river, the wind was up and it was thundering and the rain was beginning to fall. They followed real close to the bank and when they got to the camp site, they pulled the boat on the shore, off loaded the supplies and attempted to cover it with my tarp by attaching rope to small saplings. They put up the little tent and all three jumped in as the thunderstorm unleashed torrents of rain and high winds. The wind was so strong that the tarp did not keep their supplies covered, in fact, it tore some of the grommets out of the tarp.

I was relieved to find that they had weathered the storm and would be okay. Curtis had made coffee that morning and was getting ready to cook breakfast. Tom had found an old bucket and was preparing for target practice. I had a cup of coffee with them, bid them "farewell", and headed home.

Maybe next time, they will pay attention to the "old man" and be a little more concerned about the weather!

INSTRUCTIONAL

DUCKS AND DUCK CALLING

One way to learn to call ducks is to purchase a recording from some of the instructors that produce them for sale. They will demonstrate on the recording the different types of calls, high ball, comeback call, feed call lonesome hen call, etc. You can usually get these by ordering them from a mail order house, maybe some of the better sporting goods store will have them.

After getting one, go to a sporting good store and purchase several of the better known calls, but don't buy any that are too hard to blow. If you do, you cannot put any feeling or excitement into the call. When you get down to it, the very best way to learn is to observe the sounds and calls that the ducks make in their natural environment.

When you get proficient, you should be able to imitate three different mallard hens. As a novice, though, you don't want to call to often. When you get a duck or some ducks to circle, let your decoys bring them in. But after you get pretty good, you can call as much as you want.

Bear in mind if you hunt late in the evening, use your call sparingly as ducks don't really like to divulge where they are roosting. Generally, a few quacks are about all you'll need.

Forget about all that "contest type" calling. That is a waste of energy. If you try that type of calling, you will probably run all the ducks off the lake! Usually 6 or 8 quacks, followed by a few single quacks and then a few rapid quacks, and then a little "feed call" is all you need. Watch your ducks, and if they are close, let them pass before you call anymore. They can pinpoint from where you are calling.

Good Luck!

WING SHOOTING

This is especially for the beginners as the more experienced hunters possibly know about wing shooting already.

There are basically three methods of wing shooting. The first is the <u>spot shot</u>, where you basically shoot to a spot where you think the bird will be. To me, this is the least desirable although there are some hunters that do very well with this method.

Then there is the <u>follow-through</u> method, this is when you pick up your target and swing through it, firing the gun as you pass the target. I believe this is the most often used method.

The method I use most of the time is the <u>estimated lead</u>, that is, pick up your target and track it and move ahead the distance you think is necessary for your shot charge to meet the target. Bear in mind, most of the misses happen when you do not lead enough or you shoot too low. It is estimated that to hit a duck at 40 yards flying at 40 miles per hour you have to lead eight feet. The reason the lead has to be so much is because of the decrease of the velocity of the shot when they get out that distance. If you hit a duck by leading it two feet at 20 yards, you have to increase your lead four times at 40 yards as the shot charge slows down considerably.

Shooting too low is caused by the shooter seeing to much bird, especially incoming birds. There are two methods I use for incoming birds. The first method is to pick up your bird and completely cover it with your gun barrel and fire. If you can see the bird when you fire, you will shoot under it.

The next method I sometimes use is to lower the stock of your shotgun a little on your shoulder then you will see the bird but will have some lead on it.

At normal range, try to shoot incoming birds at a 45 degree angle. If they are high, this will make the range to long, you may have to shoot in a more straight up position.

On a moving target, don't aim your gun, point it. I see no use for the florescent front sights or any other color sights. Point your shotgun, lead and shoot. Don't be tentative or you'll miss.

Another thing, if you see your target approaching from a long distance, don't start tracking too soon. Wait until the bird is reasonably close, then bring your gun up, swing and fire. If you start tracking to soon, you'll have a tendency to aim.

I hope this will help some novice just starting out.

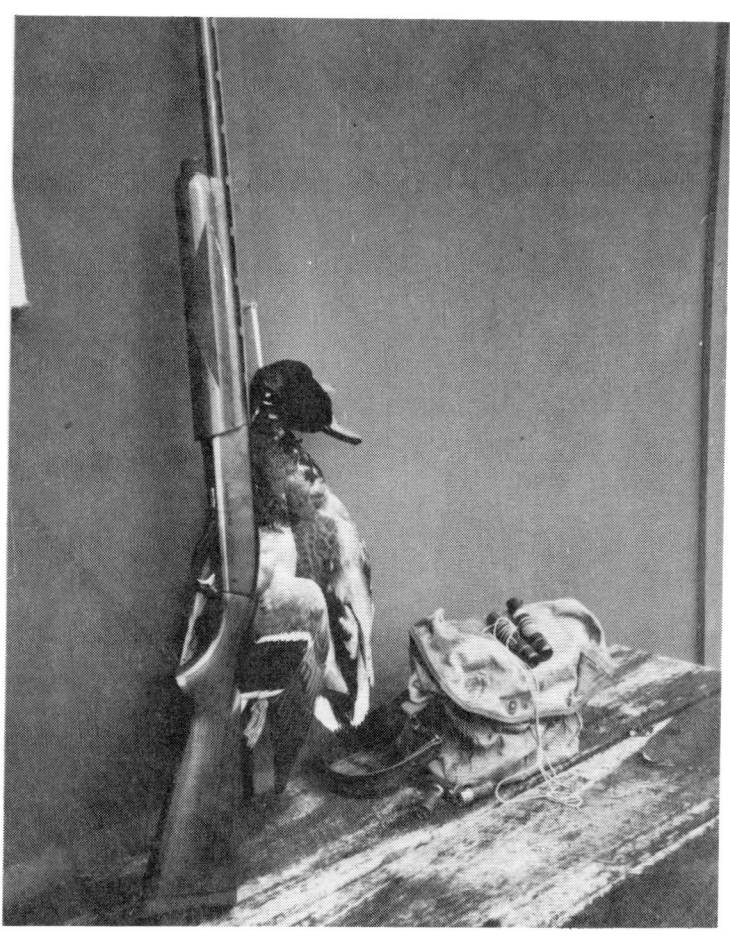

The author's gun and shell bag.

SHOTGUNS AND SHELLS

Most of the duck hunters I know use 12-gauge shotguns and most use auto loaders or pump guns. I personally use an auto loader 12-gauge with improved cylinder choke. I know very few hunters that use double or single barrel shotguns. The third shell is really necessary to avoid losing cripples.

Before the advent of steel shot, I knew of several excellent wing shots that used 20-gauge and 16-gauge guns. But the use of the steel shot stopped most of that.

A 20-gauge or 16-gauge shotgun with magnum load will do the job for ducks in close, but not for extended range. Every hunter I know despises steel shot. The range of clean kills are greatly reduced and you really have to concentrate on letting the ducks come 5 or 10 yards closer that you previously did.

Now on the market there are other types of shells with pellets that have more density than steel, but still not as dense as lead. To most hunters, the cost of these shells is prohibitive. So I say to you, let them come in closer, try to avoid losing these magnificent birds.

There is a lot written about shot size. For many years before steel shots, I used #6 high brass shells, never magnums. I had no trouble making clean kills at 40 to 45 yards. Now, after trying #2, 3 and 4 magnums, I have settled on #4's but I still use 2¾ inch shells. I haven't gone to the 3 inch shells yet and probably won't.

The advice I can give on this subject is to improve your calling, make a better blind, and decoy set and get them in close. Like that, you'll avoid a lot of cripples.

TRAINING A RETRIEVER

I will tell about the way I trained my retriever and it'll work for you.

The first thing you need to do when you get your puppy is teach it obedience. Don't start your training too early as a puppy wants to play for the first six months or so. When you start training in earnest, one of the first things you have to do is teach your dog to "sit and stay". This is most important. And the way to do this is to put a leash on your dog and lead him to a spot in the yard and command him to "sit", and when giving him this command, push down gently on his hind quarters and command "stay".

If he tries to stand, give a little tug on the leash and give him the command again and push his hind quarters down and say "sit, stay". Don't over do it. He won't do it immediately, but soon will finally get the idea. Praise him when he does stay.

Keep your training sessions short, about 15 minutes, but almost every day. You will come to enjoy it.

If you have a vantage point to observe him from without him seeing you, try this. Command him to sit and stay, then get out of his sight, around the corner of your garage or look through the window of your utility room to see if he does stay. If he doesn't stay, go out put him at the same spot, scold him and command him to "sit" and "stay". Once he has mastered this, he is ready to train.

Next, you should teach him to heel. The way to do this is to have him sit next to you, give a tug on the leash and proceed to say "heel" as you walk away. If he wants to lead rather than walk by your side, gently tap him on the muzzle with the end of the leash and command him to heel.

I find it best to use a choke collar if he begins to tug you forward. (No, a choke collar is not cruel.)

Once he has advanced to this point, it is time to start him retrieving a dummy. Always start him on land, throw the dummy and command him to "fetch" and the fun begins, he will love it. But always stop before he tires of the game.

Now it's time to go to the water. Don't throw the dummy too far at first. When he gets used to the water, you can throw it farther.

He is now ready for hand signals and this is the most difficult phase of the training. In your yard, set up an imaginary baseball diamond. Have your dog to "sit" and "stay" at the pitcher's mound location. Show him his dummy and walk to first base position and drop the dummy to the ground. Go to home plate and, with a wide motion of your arm towards first base, command him to "fetch" and at the same time saying "over, over".

Do the same thing as you did for the first base in the direction of the supposedly third base. Make your arm motions exaggerated, always let him see you drop the dummy, always say over as you waive your arm in the direction you want him to go.

The next command will be "back". To do this, let him see you drop the dummy at second base, go back to the home plate and say "back" while motioning with your arm in that direction.

To have him retrieve coming to you, drop the dummy between home plate and the pitcher's mound and command "come in, come in". It will not take long for him to associate your arm motion with the way you want him to go. What a joy you will have when your dog makes that first blind retrieve on a duck that he did not see fall.

Talking about the different breeds of retrievers, there are several good breeds and individuals have the breeds that they admire the most. I am partial to Labradors. My dog was a chocolate Lab. I used "Rusty" on all types of retrieving. In the dove field, all I had to do was pick out a spot where I wanted to shoot from, sit on my shell bucket and never have to move. Any dove that hit the ground was brought to me and I never lost a dove that I had knocked down.

I also used "Rusty" woodcock hunting and he was very good at that. He would not hold a point on a woodcock as I've heard that some Labs would do, but he would flash point. I could see when he was close to a bird and therefore could be ready to make a shot. He would also retrieve the woodcock.

So, get a retriever, take your time and train him. I always preferred a dog that was kind of like me, a little hard headed and head strong!. I do not like a dog that is shy. A dog has to be real aggressive and have a desire to fight that mud and take that cold water.

A retriever is a real valuable asset for a duck hunter. It will definitely cut down on lost cripples. I had a chocolate lab that I acquired when he was two months old. I trained him myself. Rusty was his name and he was quite a dog. It never got too tough for Rusty. I hunted the marsh one season in the 70's when the point system was in effect and you could legally bag 10 ducks if you were selective in what species you bagged. My partner and I bagged several hundred ducks that season without losing any. Rusty lived to be 16 years old. I didn't take him out his last 3 years, but when I had to have him "put down", it was a sad day. He's buried in my backyard now with a marker by his grave. I lost a good, devoted friend when I lost Rusty. His picture in on my den wall. If you have the facilities for a dog, get a retriever as they make good pets and are good hunting companions. It is not too difficult to train one.

GETTING THERE THE HARD WAY

It's about a 1/4 of a mile from the canal to the lake that I hunt and fish in and it's way too far to carry a pirogue, so I had to think of a means to do it.

I went to the a local lawnmower repair shop and purchased two solid tired, 20" lawnmower wheels. I then went to a lumber yard and got a piece of 4" x 4" lumber, approximately 30" long and then to a hardware store and there I purchased two ½" by 8" lag bolts and two pieces of flat bar 1/8" by 1½" wide by 2' long.

I drill a hole in each end of the flat bar, one hole big enough for the lag bolt to pass through and one hole for a 3/16" bolt about 3" long.

I fasten the wheels to the 4" x 4" by putting the bolt through the wheel and then through the flat bar and screwing the lag bolt into the 4" x 4", with a wheel on each end of the 4" x 4".

The flat bar is attached to the gunnels by drilling a hole in the gunnels and passing the 3/16" x 3" bolt through the flat bar and through the gunnels and then securing it with a wing nut. The flat bar should be at a slight angle of 30° degrees and the 4" x 4" is to be placed under the middle of the pirogue. When you pull the pirogue, the wheels will have a tendency to be forced to the rear and like that you don't need any other support. They will come as you pull the pirogue.

To pull the pirogue, I always use my push pole as a tongue. You secure your push pole midways the pirogue and then let possibly three feet stick out pass the bow of the pirogue and like that you could load your pirogue with your decoys, your gun and any other supplies that you needed to take with you and it's very easy to pull. If you have a path, you can pull it with one hand and I would usually pull in twice a season, once during the teal season and out again and then back in for the regular duck season and my pirogue would stay until the end of duck season. Then I would pull it out and store it for another year.

Often my fishing partner and I would come to a canal or bayou that had been plugged with an earthen dike. We had to come up with an easy way to make the pull. One method, if you were going to go over this dike often, was to purchase several links of 4" PVC pipe. We would split these pieces of pipe in half and put them round side up into the dike. You could space them several feet apart, maybe as much as three feet. This made pulling over real easy.

Another method to use if the pull is not to be frequent is to cut some green willow poles and make a mat. Green willow is very slick and will make the pull much easier.

Pirogue on wheels.

Two 5 ½ lb. "pull over" bass caught by the author.

BUILDING DIFFERENT TYPES OF DUCK BLINDS

Platform Blind:

You will need about eight four inch willows, 10 feet long, for your poles. You drive those down, four on each side. You will need four two inch by sixteen feet willow poles or any other material, I'm saying willow because that is what we usually use down here. About eight two inch by four feet willow poles, is for the cross pieces. You'll need two pieces of plywood, half inch by two feet by eight feet, the reason you cut that four by eight sheet in half lengthwise is to make it easier to handle and it is just as stable.

For the ramp, for your dog to come up and down, you'll need a 12 inch board about eight feet long and then you want to put cleats across because when a dog is wet and muddy, he cannot climb unless you have cleats for his feet to catch on.

Regarding the hardware, you'll need about 15 to 20 sixty penny nails, because one sixty penny nail through that 2 inch or 4 inch wood is enough to hold it together. And also, about a pound or so of sixteen penny nails. This blind is made to put your boat under. And what we usually use to dress a blind of that sort is whatever the local foliage is around there. We usually use willow or wax myrtle or you can use anything that grows in the vicinity because you want the blind to look as natural as possible. That usually works out real fine.

Pirogue Blind:

The next type of blind I want to describe is a pirogue blind for one man. Paddle out where you want to hunt and construct this blind and it is just suitable for one man. Some of the materials you'll need are two 2 x 4's, eight feet long and I usually use treated material. You'll need six 1x 2 eight feet long and also 12 feet of camouflage burlap material and a pound or so of roofing nails or roofing tacks.

The way to build this blind is to pick the location where you want to hunt and then drive your 2 x 4's into the bottom of the lake. Drive them just wide enough apart for your pirogue to fit in pretty snug at the middle of the pirogue. They are driven down to secure the pirogue because as you know, the pirogue get pretty tippy to shoot out of.

To stabilize it, put an eye screw in the pirogue on each side at the midpoint and have 2 six feet pieces of ¼ inch or 3/8 inch nylon rope. Then you can lash the pirogue to each one of the 2 x 4's and it then becomes relatively sturdy. The other material I mentioned, the 1 x 2's and the camouflage material is used to conceal most of the pirogue and the hunter. Cut the 12 feet material in half, you have two six feet pieces, and it runs about 48 inches or 54 inches in width. So by taking the 1 x 2's, eight feet long and stapling your camouflage to them and securing it with the roofing nails you can put one piece on each side driving the three pieces of 1 x 2 into the mud to keep the camouflage burlap extended. Put one on each side, then cut your brush to finish the blind. The burlap is just to give some "body" to the blind, if you will.

Then use whatever material you have handy to finish the concealing. The brush that you use will cover the ends of the pirogue. What I like about this blind is that it is easy to make. Another thing, if you're in a section of the lake and the ducks are not using there, you can, without too much effort, pull up those stakes, pull up your 2 x 4's and relocate for the next morning's hunt. It does not take a lot of effort to do that.

When you pull your poles up with your camouflage cloth on them, you can roll that up and put it across your pirogue and also your eight feet 2 x 4 and go to another location. Just in a matter of couple of hours, you can be relocated for the hunt the next day. That generally works out pretty good.

Boat Blind:

The next blind I want to describe is real fine, it's a boat blind, that's where the two hunters stay in the boat. The first step to constructing this blind is to pick out a place. I usually like to find a cypress tree with a lot of moss hanging on it. You want to make this blind where you construct it with the bow of your boat against the cypress tree. I'll get into more about that, but first let me list some of the materials you'll need.

You'll need eight pieces of 4" inch willow poles x 10' long, four pieces of 2" inch x 16' willow poles, about 30 feet of hog wire or chicken wire, you'll need about 15 or 20 sixty penny nails, and a pound or so of staples.

The way you build this blind is to position your boat with the front of it against a tree that has quite a bit of cover on it because that will make everything look natural. Drive the poles down into the bottom of the lake, and drive them just far enough apart to where your boat will fit in there, pretty snug. After you get the poles down, take the 16 feet poles of willow and nail them against the tree trunk, one on each side, and then to the poles you have driven into the lake bottom. With the other willow poles, you put a mid-rail. All this is put up as sort of a frame to hold the hog wire. You can use either the hog wire or chicken wire, however, I prefer the hog wire because it has four inch squares and that feature makes it easier to use. Put the hog wire on, use about 12 or 14 feet of it on each side of this frame that you've made with the willow.

Where you come in with the boat, the entrance, you make sort of a door that you can open and close to let the boat in. That's simply taking a piece of that hog wire and wiring it to one side, with a little piece of wire or rope to secure it after you get the boat inside the blind.

What you do now is gather a bunch of moss and, if you're in a cypress swamp or swamp that the trees grow this moss on, you get a boat load of moss and come back and put the moss in the holes in the wire that you have nailed to the tree and poles.

I want to tell you that moss is one of the best blind materials that you can possibly use. If you get that blind filled with moss and get a hog wire door, pull your boat in there, you'll have a real natural looking blind. It is natural as any blind you'll ever want to hunt out of.

Another thing about that moss, (people don't know this, a lot of hunters do and I guess some don't), once you put it in there and kind of string it out, it won't blow off after it gets wet and hangs on to that wire. I would suggest when you do use the moss, put it on thick and you'll have a blind for most of the season. Occasionally, you might have to add a little bit more moss, but that easily done. It's a real, real natural looking blind.

Stump Blind:

For a stump blind, you really have to find what you're looking for in a good place, in other words, it has to be on the edge of a body of water. What we usually do is look for a stump 3 feet in diameter that has hollowed out. Where a lot of logging has taken place, it's not to hard to find a stump like that. You might have to look at several until you find one that will accommodate an individual, one that you can get in. What we usually do in looking for one is to find a shell of a tree, with the shell of the tree being pretty substantial, especially if it is an old cypress tree because it appears that the middle of the stump will rot out before the outer shell for some reason. All you have to do is on the back side where you can stand in shallow water or on the edge of the swamp, pull out a slab of that wood. If it won't pull out by hand, you might have to take a hand saw and cut a slit for you to be able to go in. If it is muddy down in the middle of it, you can throw some of that material that you tore off into the bottom to stand on. Alter it to the best of your ability. Get it to where you can stand up in it, just about a little over waist high. Like that, when you're calling your ducks and have your decoys out front and you stoop down ,you're virtually invisible. That is really about the deadliest blind anybody can have to hunt ducks in.

Sometimes, it is difficult finding one but I've found them most anytime I wanted to find one. Some are a little easier to work with and some are harder. But I have found some that took very little effort to get ready to hunt and some will be dry inside.

Of course, you've got to be careful that there are not insects or spiders in there. Most of the time there are not. I've made some nice hunts, hunting out of a stump blind.

By the way, using your stump blind, if you have to get there with your pirogue, you need to pull your pirogue into some brush. What I've done previous to the morning I wanted to hunt, I cut some brush and put it on the shore or nearby there, and pull the pirogue up there and throw the brush on top of the pirogue and then walk back to the stump with my hip boots. That works pretty good. Really, a pirogue that is camouflaged the right kind of way, doesn't need very much cover to make it where it is not noticeable by the ducks.

Floating Blind:

Now I want to talk about a blind that is best used where you have water fluctuation problems. It is a floating blind. There are many kinds of floating blinds that you can build. The thing is you need to use is the material you have there to make it. I'm going to list the materials first, because there is different types of materials.

You can use logs, old timbers, discarded oil field timbers, 55-gallon drums, Styrofoam or what not, as long as the material will float your blind with a couple of people in it.

As for me, I like logs, if I can find the logs to use. The last one I built, year before last, I used logs. I was able to find five cypress logs that had been left in the swamp for many years and were still sound. I rounded up five logs from different areas of the swamp and took them to a central point. You want your logs to be at least two feet in diameter, and about 15 feet long. What you do with those logs, you lash them together. Now what I use is treated material, I use some 2 x 4 about 12 feet long. These 2 x 4's, (I use treated 2 x 4 because this is a blind you're going to keep for a good long time), they are used to hold all your logs together. You want to put the logs as close as you can to one another. There again, use some sixty penny nails and lash your raft together. And that's what it amounts to is a raft.

So far as the material for the blind itself, use just about the same material that I've used, described in making some of these other blinds. But make sure it's treated. You want to make a frame on this raft about four feet high. Use treated material for your post coming up and also for your stringers. You want a mid rail and you also want the stringers going around the blind. The only difference is most of time you're probably in water too deep for your brush to be planted down in the bottom. So around the exterior edge of the blind, up at the top rail and the bottom rail, you want to put some 2 " x 4" spacer blocks. Like that, you can put a strip of material around the blind, both top and bottom. You use those strips with the spacer blocks so you can push your brush down through there and it will keep your brush secure, because that's the only way you would have of securing brush on a blind like that.

As for the floor, you need to have a sheet of ½" inch 4 x 8 exterior plywood. You need to have some 2 x 6 on edge. You stand them on edge on top of your logs and you mount your plywood floor on top of that. The reason for that is, if you don't do that, even with five good sturdy logs, especially if you have a little wind you are going to get a little water to come on top of your logs. If you stand your 2x6 on edge, put your plywood floor on top of that, you won't have to worry about that.

What we usually do, if you have the room, you can either pull your pirogue in the blind or you can lash it to the side of the blind and let some of your blinding material cover the pirogue. When you do that, you make your opening to get in the blind on the side, so you just paddle up to the blind and let one man get out and then get out with him, tie the pirogue, then your brush coming off the of the blind will brush the pirogue.

There again, you need some sixty penny nails to drive into your stringers that hold your logs together. Then you need some ten and sixteen penny nails to build your frame made out of treated 2 x 4. Once you get it put together like that, especially made out of treated material, you'll have a blind for a number of years before you have to do anything to it. It is very good to have because you can hook your boat to it and pull it to different locations in the lake because as you know if you hunt ducks at all, they don't always use the same part of the lake and you can move and just in a matter of a couple of hours, be set up in another place and probably have some good hunting.

Natural Blind:

The next type of blind that I want to discuss, I call a natural blind. This type of blind requires very little work. Generally, a sharp machete is about all that is needed. If you can find a tree that has been blown down and continues to grow you've got it made.

All you have to do is position your pirogue among the live branches and secure it, then trim the excess foliage away. One time, I found a large willow that had been blown down practically level with the water right on the edge of a slough. We put a piece of plywood on the trunk and had a perfect blind, one we could step off of onto the shore, we called it the old log blind. Made some nice hunts from that setup.

Pirogue blind and decoys.

"Rusty" and the author on a platform blind.

BLIND PLACEMENT

Blind placement and decoy placement are both equally important to be a successful hunter, as well as the number of decoys used. I find for large bodies of water, the more decoys, the better. Always place the decoys down wind of the blind with an opening in the middle in front of the blind. Ducks do not like to come in over a blind. In a pothole, pothole hunting for mallards, 12 to 24 decoys are enough. Try not to set up where the trees are too tall around the pothole. Ducks are real reluctant to come in where it is too difficult for them to get out.

If you're hunting mostly in the morning, place your blind where the sun is at your back. In other words, face your blind to the west. It is also important to set up your blind and decoys when possible near where the ducks are using. No matter how good your blinds, calling, and decoys are, if the ducks don't want to use in that area, they will not come. One time, I had an old market hunter to tell me that he had a dozen live decoys in his spread and could not get ducks to come in when they wanted to use a different area about 200 yards away.

PUSH POLES

I want to say something about push poles. Where I hunt most of the time, you could not make it without a push pole. I make, or rather, assemble my push poles. I have been fortunate enough to acquire several fiberglass pole vaulting poles which I use for my push poles.

I go to the sporting goods store and purchase a "duck bill" to attach to the fiberglass vaulting pole. I make an adapter to attach the "duck bill" to the fiberglass pole.

I make my poles 10' long, which is longer than the length sold in stores, and bind them in several places with nylon wrapping for good hand holds so that the hand does not slip. You can be sure you will not break one of these poles.

Most of the commercial push poles are too short. You need the extra length, especially if you are in a boggy bottom.

The proper way to use a push pole is to stand up with the pole at a 45° angle. As you plant the pole, you should walk it hand over hand for at least 2 or 3 strokes, then plant it again, etc.

SWAMP (MUD) SHOES

I devised a very useful item that I call "swamp mud shoes". I came up with this invention because of a lake I frequently hunt in and fish in, where, early in the season before the rain or before high water, some of the water is so low and so shallow that there are mud banks that extend sometimes a 100 feet out before you get to water deep enough to paddle. The bottom is like quick sand and there is no way to wade out to the edge of the water, so I had to come up with a way.

I went to the local lumber yard and bought two pieces of 3/8 inch by 8 inch by 2 feet exterior plywood, and at the local hardware store I bought 18" of 4 inch wide nylon webbing, 4 feet of 1/8 inch nylon rope and also a dozen small brass bolts and washers. I fashioned a slot with the webbing on each board, midways the board, to put my hip boot foot in, much in the fashion of a water ski, one slot on each board.

I drilled two ¼ inch holes near where my heel would be, passed two feet of nylon rope through those holes and this was to tie around the ankle of my boot.

This works very well, but you have to hold on to the pirogue as you wade out and be cautious not to fall. When reaching water, I take off the "swamp mud shoes" and use them again when I'm ready to pull out . This simple, but utilitarian invention works very well for the conditions of this lake.

Caution: Never try to use these "mud shoes" without holding on to your boat or pirogue.

Swamp mud shoes.

GETTING OUT OF A MUD HOLE

I have often times tried to get from the road to a body of water and that sometimes involved going through a short section of woods. And several times in going from the road to the water hole, I've become stuck and had real difficulty getting out because it was so hard to jack up a wheel and put something under it, so I came up with this method.

All that is needed is a link of rope or chain. Chain works best as there is no stretch. You'll also need a hatchet or buck saw. The rope or chain has to be long enough to reach from the front of the car to a tree or a stump or something to secure the chain to. You need to have the hatchet or buck saw to cut a couple of saplings - one sapling could be five feet long and maybe four inches in diameter, and one possibly seven feet long and 2 ½ inches in diameter.

You place one end of the chain or rope to the vehicle bumper or axle and one end to a tree or stump and leave enough slack in the chain to take a bite to run the 7 ft. sapling through. In other words, what you're going to do is make a windlass in the center of the rope.

Now I need to say, you have to have at least two people to do this. But if you have three and on occasions I've had three, it works better. Two people can do it, however, it is more difficult. One person needs to hold the 5 ft. sapling up and the other person or persons takes the 7 ft. pole and passes it through the bite or loop, if you will, in the chain. Then you go round and round winding the chain on to the upright sapling.

Now it's no need to put the sapling in a hole. What you need to do is have the person that is holding the sapling up try to guide the chain as close as possible to the middle of the sapling. By going around, it's very easy to pull a car or truck with a little effort. If you're going to use a rope, be very careful because of the elasticity of the rope, it could possibly cause someone to get hurt.

BOAT BUILDING

In 1935, I helped my dad build a boat for a friend. He built it out of 1" x 12" cypress boards, 14' long.

You need 5 boards and several feet of 1" x 4" material for the ribs and about 1 ½ " x 12" x 4' board for the transom and a 4" x 4" piece of timber for the stem, for this is a pointed skiff.

In about 1940, we built a 12' plywood boat, 3' wide in the bottom, with 12" sides. We bought the plywood from Montgomery Wards - it was marine plywood. We used oak for the ribs. It took 2 sheets of plywood 3' x 12' x ¼" and it was a good car top boat as it weighed less than 100 pounds. We used it for a lot of years.

In 1948, when I came back from the service, I built a 14' cypress bateau. The materials were about the same except it was not pointed in design. It was very heavy, but that didn't matter as we left it in one place for several years.

Later, we had to use that boat to go up the Red River, so we extended the sides and transom 4" and used 2   5 HP motors on it to take us up that 12 miles of river. It cut our traveling time in half with that extra motor. I'd lock one motor in forward and steer with the other one. It worked out real good.

In 1952, I built a 14' pirogue out of 3/8" plywood, and I have to tell you, I have used it every year since. I don't believe this kind of plywood is available today. I used it for the 1997-98 duck season, and it is still good - 46 years old! It gets a good coat of paint about every 2 years and, during the off-season, it is kept in a good place.

In 1953, I built a 14' plywood bateau. I used oak ribs and brass screws. It was 42" wide at the bottom with 16" sides that flared out 4" on each side. I bought a 1953 25 HP Evinrude motor to put on that boat and it really worked good. We could make that long run up the Red River in 30 minutes - a far cry from the 2 hours it used to take us.

In 1958, I built a 13' runabout that I used for hunting and fishing, but I also used it in a 100-mile boat race in the Mississippi River from Greenville, MS to Vicksburg, MS. That boat was made out of 3/8" 5-ply marine plywood and white oak framing. It was a fine boat. I put 5 longitudinal stringers in the bottom. Everything was white oak. I used 12 gross of brass screws, placing the screws on 2" centers. It was a tough boat and it ran good.

Pirogue near completion.

Runabout built by the author.

LAUNCHING A BOAT AT A DIFFICULT LANDING

Several times I've launched in places where it just wasn't possible to back in far enough or you would run the risk of having your car stuck. So, I came up with a pretty good solution and this is the way it goes.

What's needed is a 2 inch rope pulley, a piece of chain and a cold shut to join the chain together. This chain should be about 2 feet long, a pretty heavy chain. You also need a piece of 3/8 inch nylon rope with a hook on one end and a spliced eye on the other. This rope should be as long as the distance from the bow eye of your boat to the pulley that you have now hooked to the chain that you have placed around the axle of your trailer. All you have to do now is place the hook that is attached to the rope into the bow eye. Put the spliced eye through the pulley that is attached to the axle, then hook the trailer. Winch to the spliced eye and by cranking the boat trailer winch, you will back the boat off the trailer with very little effort.

INSPIRATIONAL

SOLITUDE

After a restless night's sleep in my camp on the Atchafalaya River, I am awakened by the clatter of my alarm clock that was set for 4:00 a.m. Today is the opening day of duck season. I have been looking forward to this day since the close of last season.

I climb out of my warm sleeping bag and fire up the wood stove as it is pretty cold this morning. The temperature is hovering around 32° and a heavy frost is covering the ground.

I light the propane stove to make coffee and bake biscuits. After a cup of coffee and a hot biscuit, I hurriedly dress, putting on layers of clothing and hip boots, and make one last check of the articles I must take with me to the blind - duck calls, shotgun shells, etc. I go to the water's edge, untie my boat, crank up the outboard and motor across the canal to my path through the swamp.

It is pitch black and I'm about half way through my 20 minute walk, through the swamp, to where my pirogue is stashed. Without the beam of my flashlight, it is literally impossible to see my hand in front of my face. I complete my walk and I pull the pirogue to the water's edge, load my gear, and shove off. It is about an hour before dawn. The lake is like a mirror, and the silence is deafening. The only sound is the dipping of my paddle into the water as I "J-stroke" through the darkness. My light is off and I navigate by Polaris.

As I pause in my paddling, I look up and the stars seem close enough to touch. I sit there doing nothing except taking in this magnificent view of the universe.

My mind wanders and I am some place else. I think of the Indians in their canoes and Eskimos in their kayaks, both of worlds gone by, however, doing the same thing then as I am now. I am transfixed by the magnitude of the sight I am seeing and I realize the insignificance of one human being - like a grain of sand on a tremendous beach.

I don't know how long I sit. Time seems to have stood still. I cannot help but think of a supreme being that put all of this together. I am as close to Him as I'll ever be.

I am jolted back to reality as a comet blazes across the sky. I look to the East and see that the sky is lightening.

Now, back to reality, I start to paddle in haste. My duck blind is still a quarter mile away.

DEVOTION

I was motoring along with a small motor on one of the many backwoods bayous in the swamp when I came upon a pair of mallards on a log. This was late in the summer when all the mallards had departed north.

As I approached, they slid into the water. As I got closer, the drake took off, imitating a cripple duck, and the hen swam into the brush. I went along with his ruse. Every 50 yards or so, he would land on the water, then take off again, attempting to distract me from the hen. After several hundred yards, he sailed away.

I saw this pair several times that summer and I can imagine their conversation, in their low guttural sounds. She would probably say, "You better leave now, it's getting late…" and he would respond, "No, I'm going to stay with you to protect you…', knowing full well that shortly he would begin to molt and be flightless, thus susceptible to predators - just like her.

I have seen a wounded mallard glide out of a flock and then another mallard, possibly the mate, glide down beside her. I don't know if mallards are monogamous, but I do know that they "pair up" before heading north.

There are hunters, some of whom I know, who will not hunt the speckle belly geese any more as it is a fact that this species is monogamous.

I need not dwell on this subject too long.

LAST DAY OF A SEASON

I guess it was about 1970 when my old friend, Mr. Mack, and me, were breaking camp on the arm of Grand Lake. It was the last day of the duck season.

We would always take down the tent each weekend during the season, but we would leave the cook fly standing, ready for the next weekend; however, this weekend was different. We were taking everything in.

Mr. Mack was 24 years my senior and, on this occasion, he remarked about this being a sad occasion as he didn't know how many more seasons he was going to have.

Now that I'm about the age he was then, I get the same feeling and, sitting here reflecting on different things, I can appreciate his feelings.

Who knows, maybe I have a few more seasons, and maybe not, but we will just take it as it comes. No need to dwell on something of which we have no control. When you are young, this is the furthest thing from your mind, but the day will come and you, too, will get the feeling.

My old partner, Mr. Mack, getting ready to take a little "nip" <u>after</u> the hunt.

LAST HUNT OF THE SEASON

I was paddling my pirogue out of the swamp on the last morning of the season. I would not hunt anymore this season, and that day, I had not limited out. I need 2 more mallards.

The weather was too bright and calm, and the ducks had become very wary after 60 days of hunting. I figured if I paddled the "flooded 4 wheeler trail", I might get a jump shot, as there was no obstruction to make noise and I was taking it real easy.

I had my auto loader across my knees and was about 200 yards from where I would take the pirogue out of the water. All of a sudden a pair of mallards leaped to the air to my right and cut across in front of my pirogue. That green head of the drake was shining in the mid-morning sun.

I was on them in a flash for what would have been two easy shots, but I lowered my gun without shooting and said to myself, "God speed, you beautiful creatures, I hope you make it back up north safely."

As I pulled my pirogue up on the bank and secured it, and started walking the trail back to the camp, I had a warm glow. A smile came across my mouth, and I thought to myself, "You old son-of-a-gun, you have mellowed."

I had a good season.

"DAYS GONE BY"

In the past, I've had the opportunity to have a few good hunting partners, and by the way, good hunting partners are hard to come by. Some are still around, but for one reason or another - usually age-they don't hunt anymore and some are not with us anymore as they have passed on.

I think about my old hunting partners especially when I'm in a duck blind waiting for daylight and the time to shoot. I hope they are in a better place where those beautiful birds decoy every time and they always make a good shot. I am 75 years old now and don't know how many more seasons I'll have to hunt, but I hope I have a few.

My old hunting partner, Mr. Mack said, "Bud, I don't know if you can feel my presence in that duck blind, but I am with you."

I've hunted for over 60 years. Most of it duck hunting. I've had my share of good luck. I've been able to bag 15 banded ducks, one of which had been banded for 10 years. I also bagged a mallard muscovey hybrid which I had mounted and is now on my den wall. I also bagged 3 banded mallards in one day - all within my legal limit! I have never heard of anyone else accomplishing this feat - that was quite a stroke of luck.

When the time comes that I can't hunt anymore, I'll have no regrets. I have enough memories to last a lifetime!

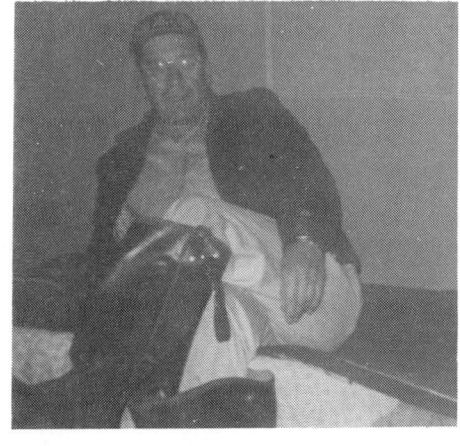

The author waiting to leave the tent for the morning hunt.

REFLECTIONS

As I look back on the writing of this book, I think about all the joyous days I have had in the out of doors, and recalling these events has greatly benefited me.

I think back on the hundreds of day breaks and the scores of dusks that I have witnessed, the happiness and anticipation of the coming day and the sadness of the last light of day, knowing that day is gone forever.

I think of all the people I have encountered on my outings and they are vivid in my mind. I see myself, in my mind's eye, as I journey from adolescence to a ripe age.

It is hard to comprehend why it is difficult to remember a recent happening and yet, easy to remember, in vivid detail, things that happened decades ago - the first fish caught, the color of the lure, the first dove or duck bagged, the exact circumstance, who I was with, the time of day.

I look back on the taking of game - am I justified in doing this? I'm sure their life is as precious to them as mine is to me. I try to justify this by saying that they must be harvested or they will over populate. I wonder.

In my youth, I always tried to "get my limit", but now, things are different. Now, the catching of one fish can be a successful trip - the way it hit the lure, the way it broke water trying to "throw the lure": the way that duck responded to my call and came in to the decoys picture perfect, that one duck would make it a successful day of duck hunting.

Today, with the increase of hunters and fishermen taking to the fields and streams, it is more important than ever to take what you can use and leave the rest to propagate the species.

I hope that whoever reads this book will get as much pleasure from it as I have had in writing it.

CAMP COOKING

The author cooking breakfast at his camp for his friend, Fred Warteman, visiting from Eau Claire, Wisconsin.

CAMP COOKING

I need to record now some of the dishes if you will or food I have cooked at the camp and also at the tent, using a tent for a camp. So, what I'm going to do, I'll give the ingredients first and then I'll try to make a blow by blow of the way I did this, and it usually turned out pretty good. These are a few of the dishes that I cook in the woods. They are pretty simple, don't take a lot of equipment, or a lot of ingredients. Most of the time they'll come out fairly good, especially if you've had a hard day in the field and are pretty hungry, they even taste better. Try these and I'll think you'll enjoy them, too.

CAMP STEW:
1 onion finely chopped
¼ bell pepper
2 ribs of celery also finely chopped
1 pound of smoke sausage -1/8 inch slices
4 medium Irish potatoes cubed
1 can of Rotel diced tomatoes and chilies
1 can of tomato sauce-small
1 can of chicken broth, 15 oz.,
½ teaspoon garlic powder
½ teaspoon of Lea & Perrin Worcestershire
salt and pepper to taste

Use black iron pot for this dish and what I usually do and I'll try and keep it in the proper prospective. Put a little cooking oil in the bottom of the pot and sauté' your onions with the smoke sausage, when the onions are sautéed, add your chopped celery, bell pepper into the pot and the can of chicken broth., then add the cubed potatoes, the Rotel and the tomato sauce also a dash of Worcestershire sauce. You may now need to add some water cook on low fire, have it come to a boil and cut back to a simmer, also add the garlic powder, salt and pepper season to taste. Now if you want a milder taste rather than a spicy taste, do not put the liquid from the Rotel in the pot. Now this dish needs to cook for about an hour or hour and a half or until the potatoes are tender. I find it best to serve over hot rice. Generally this amount of ingredients will feed four people.

CORN SOUP:
1 onion, ¼ bell pepper, 2 ribs of celery all finely chopped
2 cans of creamed style corn-15 oz
2 medium Irish potatoes cubed
1 pound of medium shrimp de-veined and halved
1 small can of Rotel tomatoes
1 can of chicken broth-15 oz.
½ teaspoon garlic powder
several dashes of Lea & Perrin Sauce
salt and pepper to taste.

For this Corn Soup, I usually use about a 4-quart saucepan. I start off with a little cooking oil in the bottom and I usually use canola Oil for all my cooking. I sauté my onions, then add the celery and peppers, the chicken broth, the Rotel, the cubed potatoes, the garlic powder, the Worcestershire sauce salt and pepper to taste. After adding the garlic powder, salt and pepper, I add the creamed style corn. Add the shrimp about 20 minutes before serving. I also serve this dish over rice and it will serve four people. Incidentally, for this dish, do not add the liquid from the Rotel, it makes this soup a little bit too spicy.

FRIED FISH AND FRIED POTATOES:
2 lbs.. of fileted fish, I prefer bass but you can use any fish
3 large Idaho potatoes
1 cup of yellow corn meal
1 teaspoon of onion powder
1 teaspoon of garlic powder
½ teaspoon of cayenne pepper
½ teaspoon of salt

Mix your corn meal, salt, pepper, onion powder, garlic powder, and cayenne powder together, mix it thoroughly. Then put enough oil in the skillet or pot to cover the fish when you put the fish in the pot and bring it to a high heat. Take your fish filets and coat them with the mixture I have just described. Shake off the excess mixture and place them in to the hot oil. Fry until the fish floats and turn them over one time. After your fish is fried remove from the pan and put on paper towels. The large Irish potatoes should be cut long ways into 6 or 8 long slices. Coat them in the same mixture that you coated the fish filets and fry these until they are tender to the touch of a fork. They will have a brown coating on the outside and a soft texture inside. This also feeds four people.

PEAS AND EGGS:
8 medium eggs
2 cans of English peas-15 oz
½ stick of margarine
½ teaspoon of onion powder
½ teaspoon of garlic powder
salt and pepper to taste

For this dish you need to use a large diameter sauce pan. What you want to do is pour the English peas in the sauce pan with the liquid in the can also, then add the margarine, onion powder, garlic powder and salt and pepper. Simmer this over a low heat for about 20 minutes. If you don't have enough liquid that came in the cans with the peas you may have to add a little water. When this begins to simmer, break your eggs individually in the peas, but be careful not to break the yolk, let them poach in this mixture of peas and spices that I've named until the yolks are firm. This will also serve four people. It is a great Lenten Friday dish when some people do not want to eat meat.

SMOTHERED POTATOES AND SAUSAGE:
8 medium Irish potatoes
2/3 lbs., smoked sausage
½ small onion, finely chopped
½ teaspoon of garlic powder
1/4 cup of green onions finely chopped
salt and pepper to taste

Take the Irish potatoes and slice them real thin also slice the smoke sausage thin. Place in the pan with a little water as the potatoes have a lot of water in them, add salt, pepper, chopped onion and garlic powder. Bring to a boil and reduce the heat to a simmer. When potatoes are tender, add the green onions. Cook until most of the water is gone, stirring frequently. To enhance the flavor, let the mixture of potatoes slightly stick to the bottom of the pot. Be cautious not to burn but they will have a browning effect. Be sure and do not have your potatoes come out like creamed potatoes, they still need to be slightly firm. This dish also serves four people.

VENISON TENDERLOIN:
2 lbs.. of tenderloin sliced ½ inch thick
½ cup of plain flour
½ teaspoon each of salt and black pepper

Pour enough cooking oil in the skillet to cover the tenderloins and bring to a high heat. Mix flour, salt and black pepper thoroughly. Coat the tenderloin medallions I call them in the flour mixture, shake off the excess flour, fry rapidly in oil on high heat, drain on paper napkins.

VENISON BACK STRAP:
3 lbs. of Venison Back Straps
½ medium onion
4 cloves of garlic
½ teaspoon salt
½ teaspoon of black pepper
½ teaspoon of cayenne pepper
½ cup of red wine

This is pan baked, and I usually fix this for sandwiches. Stuff roast in a number of places with slivers of onion and garlic, sprinkle with salt, black pepper and cayenne and rub on generously. Put enough oil in the skillet or pot to cover the bottom, sear roast on all sides, add one cup of water and one cup of red wine. Reduce heat to low and cover pot. Add water as needed. Cook for approximately 1-1/2 hours. Remove pot cover and cook for 20 minutes or until tender. Let roast cool and slice.

CRAWFISH OR SHRIMP STEW:
2 lbs. or crawfish or shrimp de-veined
1 onion
¼ bell pepper
2 ribs of celery
1 small can of tomato sauce
1 can of chicken broth-15 oz.
1 small can of Rotel
a few dashes of LEA & PERRIN
½ teaspoon garlic powder
1 bay leaf
salt and pepper to taste
flour to make a roux

I make my roux by adding equal parts of flour and cooking oil into a black pot and cook this over a low heat and stir constantly. You cook this roux and for a dish such as crawfish or shrimp, you don't have to make it to dark, but I like to get a light color to the roux. When your roux is done and to the color that you like it, usually a light chocolate color, add your onions, sauté your onions, then add your celery, peppers and chicken broth, also add your Rotel, tomato sauce, 1 bay leaf, large bay leaf or 2 small bay leaves, dash of Worcestershire, salt and pepper to taste. Bring to a boil and cut down to a simmer. I like to cook this about 2 hours, add the shrimp or crawfish about 20 minutes before you are ready to serve. Be sure to remove the bay leaf from the dish. I also serve this over rice and this will serve four people.

PRESSURE POT DUCK:
2 duck breasts
1 can of tomato paste
½ onion
4 cloves of garlic
½ teaspoon of sugar
salt and pepper to taste

This is one of our favorites when we were camping out in a tent because it was relatively easy to cook, and didn't take a lot of time. Cut duck breasts into quarters and stuff each piece with slivers of onion and garlic. Cover the bottom of the 4-quart pressure pot with cooking oil. Brown the quarters on all sides, then remove from the pot. Lower heat and spoon in the small can of tomato paste, stir continuously until tomato paste turns dark, add water, reintroduce duck pieces, add ½ teaspoon sugar, place lid on pressure pot and cook for 45 minutes at 15 lbs. pressure. I also serve this over rice or spaghetti and it serves two people.

BISCUITS WITH NO OVEN:

The next thing I want to do is tell about baking biscuits when you do not have an oven available such as cooking out in a tent or a camp where you just have the small 2-burner propane stove. What's needed in this instance is about a number 10 black iron pot with a lid. I use can biscuits either 5 to a can or 10 all depending on the size of the black pot that you're going to bake them in. I take the black pot and put it on the stove at a good heat, a medium or a little above and preheat the pot for 10 minutes. I have a couple pieces of angle iron. I have two pieces bent in a 90 degree that are an inch and a half thick in other words they'll keep your pan that you're going to put your biscuits in from being on the bottom of the pot that you're baking your biscuits in because if you don't do this you'll burn your biscuits on the bottom. Well, after I have my black iron pot heating for 10 minutes, I put the biscuits in and put the lid on then I let it go for another 10 minutes turn the biscuits over because they will always brown on the bottom first. Turn them over put your lid back on your pot and go for an additional 10 minutes. At the end of that time, your biscuits will be completely done. So it takes 30 minutes to bake the biscuits in this fashion.

HAM STEAK & RED EYE GRAVY
2 lbs of ham steak, quartered
4 medium potatoes
2 carrots, cut in 1" lengths
½ small onion
½ tsp. Garlic power
½ tsp. Worchestershire Sauce
½ tsp. Cayenne pepper
¼ tsp. Black pepper
1 Tbsp. plain flour

Cover bottom of black iron pot with cooking oil. Saute' minced onions until clear. Add ham steak quarters and cook until lightly browned. Add potatoes and carrots and enough water to cover. Add seasonings. Cover pot and reduce heat and let simmer. When more liquid is needed, dissolve 1 Tbs. of flour in a cup of water and stir in. Cook until vegetables are tender. Serve over toast or instant grits. Serves (4).

RICE:

I need to say a little bit about the way I cook my rice. If you're going to cook rice for four people, I usually use a cup of rice and I use a sauce pan that will hold a sizable amount of water, because I do not steam my rice, I boil it. What you do is you put your sauce pan with your water on your fire, add some salt not to much and about a tablespoon of olive oil is what I use. I bring that water to a boil, I put the rice in and stir it and do not cover the pot and let it cook for 20 minutes. At the end of 20 minutes, I drain it into a colander and you'll find that all the grains will be separate, you'll have no sticking rice. That is the way that I cook rice.

ROUX:

I also wanted to mention something about the roux that I spoke about. Now I said use equal parts, well the more ingredients you're going to have to cook, the more roux you're going to need. Generally for a crawfish stew or shrimp stew use about an ounce of oil and the same amount of flour and then proceed to brown it the way I described earlier.

CAMP CHILI:
1 ½ lbs. of course, ground lean beef
½ medium onion, finely diced
¼ bell pepper, finely diced
1 small can tomato sauce
1 can Rotel tomatoes, diced
½ teaspoon garlic powder
½ teaspoon cayenne pepper
½ teaspoon Worcestershire Sauce
salt & pepper to taste

Canola cooking oil

Pour enough cooking oil to cover the bottom of the pot. Sauté onions and peppers until clear. Put ground beef in pot and stir until slightly brown. Add the tomato sauce and Rotel. Cook for a few minutes, then add the remaining ingredients. Bring all to a boil and cut the heat back to a slow simmer. Add water as needed. Cover pot and cook for 1 ½ hours. This dish serves four.

Bass filets ready for the skillet.

EPILOGUE

I have hunted and fished for more than 60 years. While growing up, I went with my Dad whenever possible.

After my stint in the service, I was fortunate to get a job where I would have 2 days off per week. I managed to go hunting or fishing on one of those days, Saturday, as Sunday is a church day. I was also able to make a number of trips while on vacation.

Since I have been retired for 19 years, I have been able to choose any day that I wished to go.

The outdoors are a wonderful place! Go and enjoy it, conserve it, and most importantly, leave it clean for the generations to come.